THE BASICS

OF FINANCE

Financial Tools for Non-Financial Managers

BRYAN **E. M**ILLING

SOURCEBOOKS **T**RADE
NAPERVILLE, **I**LLINOIS

Copyright © 1991 by Bryan E. Milling

Published by:

Sourcebooks Trade

A Division of Sourcebooks, Inc.
P.O. Box 372
Naperville, Illinois, 60566
(708) 961-2161
FAX: 708-961-2168

Editorial: Ellen Slezak
Design and Production: Monica Paxson
Cover Design: Concialdi Design

This publication is designed to provide accurate and authoritative information in regard to the subject matter covered. It is sold with the understanding that the publisher is not engaged in rendering legal, accounting, or other professional service. If legal advice or other expert assistance is required, the services of a competent professional person should be sought.
From a Declaration of Principles Jointly Adopted by a Committee of the American Bar Association and a Committee of Publishers and Associations

Library of Congress Cataloging-in-Publication Data

Milling, Bryan E.
   The basics of finance : financial tools for non-financial managers
/   Bryan E. Milling.
      p.   cm.
   Includes bibliographical references and index.
   ISBN 0-942061-25-X (hardcover) -- ISBN 0-942061-18-7 (pbk.)
   1. Business enterprises--Finance. 2. Financial statements.
3. Ratio analysis. I. Title.
HG4026.M55   1991
658.15--dc20   90-27684
                                                                    CIP

Printed and bound in the United States of America.
10 9 8 7 6 5 4 3 2

Contents

Contents

Section Three: Component Analysis

Section Four: Structural Analysis

Section Five: Profit Planning and Financial Forecasting Formulas

Introduction

Effective financial management remains essential for business success. But financial management typically remains the last concern for independent business managers.

Instead, they concentrate on their special interest or expertise—sales or engineering or manufacturing—and turn to the financial aspects of the business only when a crisis develops. A manager may then become uneasy or intimidated when working with the analytical tools essential for effective financial management, making decisions that influence the profitability, and perhaps the survival, of the business using information he or she doesn't fully understand.

The Basics of Finance: Financial Tools for Non-Financial Managers provides a remedy for that problem. The book can be used as a primary source for the important formulas and ratios that serve as the basic tools for business financial analysis. The glossary offers concise definitions for terms used throughout the book. The index will help you locate analytic tools quickly. But business financial management requires interpretation as well as calculation, and the book proceeds beyond the basic arithmetic to help you understand and use the data that result from your calculation.

- Is a three-to-one debt-to-equity ratio satisfactory for your business?

- How does inventory turnover rate affect your firm's financial structure?

- How does your sales volume relate to your need for working capital?

As the book helps you answer such questions, you will find that financial analysis is more than an interesting arithmetic exercise. You will find numerous examples that illustrate the major principles of financial analysis and the potential benefits from attentive financial management. Those examples will help you profit by applying the principles to your own circumstances.

You also will find many of the major tenets of financial management crystallized in a set of concise Financial Facts. For example, one Financial Fact marks the current ratio that usually represents adequate liquidity in a business. Another relates financing costs to the return on a firm's assets. Still another emphasizes the value of prompt trade payment practices.

Unique business circumstances often qualify the management tenets set forth in many Financial Facts, but collectively they provide the foundation for effective financial management of a business enterprise.

To illustrate, we will summarize the primary justification for the book.

FINANCIAL FACT 1:

Financial management is critical to the success of every business.

The book doesn't reveal any secrets, but it should become a profitable management tool whether you use it only as an occasional reference or as a primary guide for making financial decisions.

Section 1

Financial Management

Chapter 1

The Need for
Financial Management

A business may survive with haphazard financial management, but rarely will it prosper. Haphazard financial management inevitably will damage a firm's earning. The firm will earn less than it could if it relied on sound financial management principles.

From the other perspective, the business that uses the principles of modern financial management properly can increase its earnings. This chapter establishes the critical role that financial management plays in the operation of a business. That effort, or the lack of it, influences every significant aspect of a firm's operating results.

Financial analysis, the foundation for financial management, provides the basis for sensible financial management decisions. That analysis enables a business manager to understand the present financial circumstances and project future prospects. Any business manager who ignores the need for financial analysis confronts the constant threat of financial trauma.

Fulcrum of Financial Management

Almost every business activity affects a firm's financial circumstances. For example, when a business uses trade credit to buy inventory, the firm's assets and liabilities increase simultaneously. The increase in liabilities raises the firm's debt-to-equity ratio, creates a claim on future cash flow, and possibly reduces its credit worthiness.

Alternatively, when a business generates an open-account sale, it exchanges inventory for a customer's promise to pay later—an account receivable. Initially, no cash changes hands.

Collecting accounts receivable—not sales—becomes the primary source of cash for a business. Regardless of its sales volume, a business must collect its receivables to obtain the cash necessary to retire accounts payable, service fixed-debt obligations, and meet payroll. Moreover, these interrelationships become more complex as a business grows.

An increase in sales means that a firm's assets increase proportionately. A similar increase in the combined total of equity and liabilities must balance the asset expansion. The business that fails to see the need for that balance can find itself in the midst of a financial crisis. It may exhaust its cash reserves and lose the ability to meet its obligations on time. In the worst circumstance, the profitable promise anticipated from growth can lead to financial failure. Clearly, financial management requires a perpetual balancing act, as shown in Figure 1-1.

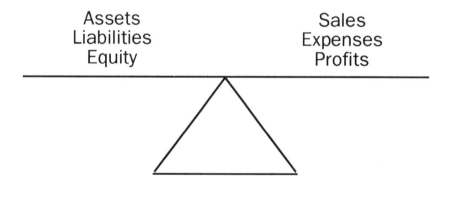

Fig. 1-1. The fulcrum of financial management.

One side of the fulcrum recognizes that a business must incur expenses to generate sales. The difference between sales and expenses become profits for the firm. The profits then increase the stockholders' equity. The other side of the fulcrum shows that a business must carry assets to generate sales. To carry those assets, it typically must use some borrowed funds—liabilities—in conjunction with the stockholders' equity. Whenever the elements resting in the fulcrum become unbalanced, a business will encounter financial problems.

For example, excess asset expansion leads to an increase in liabilities relative to stockholders' equity. The increase may make it difficult for a business to meet its obligations on time. The larger debt burden increases the risk of financial failure. At the same time, the larger debt burden inevitably increases the firm's interest costs. The business finds it more difficult to generate the earnings necessary to restore the proper balance between its liabilities and equity.

Alternatively, a business often has to incur a significant increase in expenses to encourage higher sales. Should the sales not follow as anticipated, the firm may suffer a loss that drains the stockholders' equity and upsets the balance in the firm's financial system.

In any circumstance, a business must maintain the proper financial balance to maximize its profits and ensure its survival. That balance does not occur spontaneously. It requires knowledgeable financial analysis and positive financial management.

Need for Financial Analysis

Financial analysis provides the foundation for sound financial management. It translates the conceptual relationships in Figure 1-1 into a numerical language useful for practical interpretation. After all, you can't base realistic decisions on a conceptual view of the financial interrelationships in a business. You must define that relationship with some precision.

Financial analysis makes two critical contributions to financial management: it assesses the relationships among the elements that make up the financial structure in a business; and it provides the criteria for gauging a firm's operating results.

The assessment centers on the assets, liabilities, and stockholders' equity found in a firm's balance sheet. It includes these questions:

Does a business have too much debt relative to its equity?

Or does its low debt level reduce the potential return on stockholders' equity?

5

In the first circumstance, the business incurs increased risk of financial failure. In the second circumstance, stockholders earn less than they could.

Financial analysis also evaluates the relationships between a firm's assets and liabilities. Again, that evaluation helps ensure that the firm maintains a sensible balance on the fulcrum of financial management. This promotes the firm's profitability and survival.

Sound financial analysis will then provide the criteria for gauging results. Although any measure of that performance begins with a look at the firm's bottom line, the financial performance in a business cannot be gauged by earnings alone. Earnings must also be related to the stockholders' equity and to total assets. These relationships provide a measure of how efficiently a business employs the funds at its disposal. In fact, those measures should orient any financial management effort.

Whichever gauges you employ, limiting any analysis to the current year's operation still does not properly assess your financial performance. Indeed, you must compare the current year's results with those generated in previous years. Then, you should compare your operating performance against that exhibited by similar firms in your industry.

Positive Financial Management

Fundamental financial analysis is not an intellectual province reserved for sophisticated business managers and scholars. Anyone who has some familiarity with basic accounting statements can grasp the essential concepts. But many business managers overlook this fact. They use financial analysis only when a problem arises.

A cash shortage may force a close look at an excess investment in accounts receivable. The inability to meet debt obligations promptly may encourage a look at the term structure of the firm's liabilities. Or the failure to obtain increased trade credit may raise a concern about supplier payment habits.

In any event, the premise that orients the *Basics of Finance* asserts that financial management should not remain a peripheral management concern. Nor should a manager ignore business finance until a crisis arises. An effective business manager uses the principles of financial management consistently to contribute profitably to the firm's objectives.

6

Positive financial management can make a significant contribution not only to ensuring profits, but to help ensure business survival. Every business incurs risk while seeking profits, and the drive for higher profits inevitably raises the risk. The more risk a business accepts, the higher the return it can achieve.

At the same time, risk represents a direct threat to business survival. The higher the level of the risk, the greater the threat. Realistically, a business should balance the risk it accepts with the profit it seeks. Too much risk relative to the potential return doesn't make financial sense.

Positive financial management recognizes the trade-off between the risk and return associated with every management decision. The goal that it can help bring about is to increase earnings without incurring serious risks. These objectives are emphasized here:

FINANCIAL FACT 2:

Positive financial management increases earnings and reduces the risk of financial failure.

Of course, objectives other than earnings remain important. Some business managers consider a larger sales volume the most important business objective. Others seek a larger market share. Still others may consider technological advances most significant. Yet achieving any of these objectives does not ensure profitability or survival. Orienting a business primarily toward any one of those objectives can make its operations unprofitable and its survival unlikely.

Chapter 2

Assessing a Firm's Financial Condition

Accounting convention divides the total claims on a firm's assets into two categories—liabilities and owner's or stockholders' equity. Liabilities due to creditors represent the priority claim on a firm's assets. Should a business dissolve, creditors have the first right to the proceeds gained from selling the assets. The stockholders' equity represents a secondary or residual claim on assets. In the event a business ceases operations, stockholders stand behind the creditors. They are entitled only to the proceeds from the residual assets that remain after satisfying creditor claims.

The basic accounting relationship recognizes the two categories of claims on assets:

$$\text{Assets} = \text{Liabilities} + \text{Stockholders' Equity}$$

The total assets in a business equal the total that comes from adding its liabilities to the stockholders' equity. The two totals still balance. This fundamental accounting equation provides the foundation for the construction of a business balance sheet. For example, assume that on 12/31/90 the Sample Corporation owned $500,000 in total assets. On the same date, creditors' claims on those assets totaled $250,000; stockholders held an equal (although secondary) claim on the same assets.

The basic accounting equation presents the firm's financial image in the form of a balance sheet:

The Sample Corporation
12/31/90 Balance Sheet

Total Assets	$500,000
Total Liabilities	$250,000
Stockholders' Equity	250,000
Liabilities and Equity	$500,000

Total assets still equal the total that comes from adding the liabilities to the stockholders' equity.

But the Sample Corporation's simple balance sheet provides little information useful for practical financial management. The statement tells us nothing about the specific composition of the firm's assets. Nor does it identify the nature of its liabilities.

The corporation may be financially sound, or it may lack the capability to pay its debts promptly. Either potential exists, even though a business with equity equal to its liabilities usually enjoys a comfortable financial position. You must properly categorize a firm's assets and liabilities to obtain a clear view of its financial condition.

On the left side of the equation, accountants separate a firm's assets into one of two categories. One category includes all current assets. The major current assets usually include cash, accounts receivable, and inventory. Current assets continuously revolve through the firm—a business uses cash to purchase inventory, often using trade credit to defer payment. In some circumstances, sales convert inventory directly back into cash. Then the process repeats itself.

However, most business sales are made in exchange for accounts receivable, requiring a business to wait ten to thirty days or longer for the actual cash payment for each customer's purchase. Whatever the circumstance, current assets normally revolve through a business several times during a year. The cash to inventory to accounts receivable to cash transition constantly repeats itself.

In contrast, property, machinery, and equipment a business owns stand as fixed assets. They represent a permanent investment necessary to carry on operations. Fixed assets can also revolve. More efficient machinery and equipment may replace that made obsolete by age or new technology. But fixed assets typically revolve slowly through a business, so that at a particular time accountants consider the assets permanent.

The comparative liquidity distinguishes the two categories of assets. Liquidity provides a relative measure of how easily a business can convert an asset into the cash necessary to meet its obligations. The easier the conversion, the more liquid the asset. Current assets typically demonstrate a high degree of liquidity. Of course, cash itself sets the standard. An ample cash balance insures that a business can meet its obligations promptly.

Accounts receivable usually come next on the scale of relative liquidity. Collections continuously convert a portion of a firm's receivables into cash. The typical business collects all of its existing receivables every thirty to forty-five days.

Inventory remains the least liquid current asset. After all, a business must generate a sale to convert any inventory into cash. If the sale is made in exchange for an account receivable, the business receives no cash until the customer fulfills a promise to pay. Nevertheless, an aggressive sales effort still can convert inventory into cash in a relatively short period.

In contrast, fixed assets exhibit almost no liquidity. From one perspective, they are necessary for a firm's operations. Selling the assets to generate cash isn't a realistic consideration. From another perspective, a business usually finds it difficult to sell any fixed assets at a fair price within a reasonable time. Managers view fixed assets as a permanent investment, not a source of funds to pay creditors.

To emphasize the distinction between current assets and fixed assets, on the following page we'll take a closer look at the $500,000 in total assets the Sample Corporation owned at 12/31/90.

The Sample Corporation has $375,000 in liquid assets that it probably can convert into cash within a relatively short period. Completely converting all current assets into cash becomes necessary only when a business ceases operations. Nevertheless, creditors (and stockholders) usually view all of the current assets in a business as a potential source of funds to retire its existing liabilities.

The corporation also has $125,000 in fixed assets. Those assets—a

---

The Sample Corporation
12/31/90 Balance Sheet

Cash	$ 50,000	
Accounts Receivable	175,000	
Inventory	150,000	
Total Current Assets		$375,000
Factory Building	$ 75,000	
Machinery and Equipment	50,000	
Total Fixed Assets		$125,000
Total Assets		$500,000

---

small factory building, machinery, and equipment—represent the permanent investment necessary for the firm's operations. The cash value held in those assets may be more or less than the accounting value included on the balance sheet. However, any difference in valuation remains relatively unimportant since the Sample Corporation needs the assets to continue operations. No business voluntarily sells its fixed assets to pay creditors.

On the other side of the accounting equation, a balance sheet also separates a firm's liabilities into two categories. One category includes current, or short-term, liabilities, the other deferred, or long-term liabilities.

Current liabilities include all obligations payable within the next twelve months. Those obligations usually have a close relationship to a firm's current assets. Thus, accounts payable to trade creditors for inventory purchases represent current liabilities normally due within thirty days or less. Short-term loans from banks or other lenders also represent current liabilities. Such loans typically supplement supplier trade credit and help support the borrower's investment in current assets. Similarly, the business repays such loans from the cash gained from liquidating a portion of those assets.

Deferred liabilities represent obligations that will not come due within the year following the date of the balance sheet. The business temporarily defers repayment of those obligations. Businesses can incur liabilities that require repayment on a monthly schedule that covers a number of years, but all payments due in the upcoming year qualify as current liabilities. The rest of the obligation remains a long-term liability. A look at another portion of the Sample Corporation's balance sheet illustrates the distinction between current and deferred liabilities.

The Sample Corporation
12/31/90 Balance Sheet

Accounts Payable	$100,000	
Note Payable	50,000	
Other Current Liabilities	25,000	
Total Current Liabilities		$175,000
Long-Term Liabilities		75,000
Total Liabilities		$250,000
Capital Stock	$100,000	
Retained Earnings	150,000	
Total Stockholders' Equity		$250,000
Equity and Liabilities		$500,000

On 12/31/90 creditors held $175,000 in current claims on the Sample Corporation's assets. The firm has to generate the funds necessary to satisfy those obligations during 1991 or risk financial embarrassment. At the same time, it can defer any immediate action on the $75,000 in long-term liabilities. None of those liabilities comes due before 1992. Of course, the $175,000 in current liabilities are not all immediately due and payable. But look at the $100,000 in accounts payable. Chances are that those obligations come due in the first thirty days of the year.

Accounts payable usually revolve in the same way as current assets do. The business retires accounts payable as they fall due on a day-to-day basis. Then it makes purchases that create new payables. Of course, accounts payable revolve only so long as the business pays the maturing obligations on time. Suppliers soon stop selling to the business that falls too far past due.

The Sample Corporation also has a $50,000 note payable classified as a current liability. The note presumably represents a bank loan that helps support the current assets. While the liability is current, payment may not be required until several months into the year. Moreover, such loans commonly are renewed or rolled over. So the note draws less immediate attention than the Sample Corporation's accounts payable.

Those obligations lumped together as "other current liabilities" typically attract less attention. Such obligations usually include the current portion of a firm's deferred debt, as well as short-term, recurring liabilities accrued in the normal course of business. We can assume that the Sample Corporation's 12/31/90 balance sheet properly recognizes accrued payroll, taxes, or interest expenses among the other current liabilities.

This slice from the Sample Corporation's balance sheet also categorizes the basic elements that make up the stockholders' claims on assets. The $100,000 in capital stock represents the stockholders' actual cash investment in the firm. In addition, earnings retained in the business since inception—that is, those not paid out as dividends—total $150,000. Although left in the business, those earnings represent an increase in the accounting value of each share of stock held by an investor.

Categorizing the asset, liability, and stockholders' equity accounts still doesn't provide a complete picture of a firm's financial position. That picture appears only when those accounts are combined into the traditional balance-sheet format. The Sample Corporation's balance sheet in Table 2-1 enables us to interrelate these elements.

The nature of the financial relationships in the Sample Corporation's balance sheet illustrates some critical questions for a financial manager.

What is the relationship between the firm's debt and equity? Is either one too large relative to the other? Too much debt relative to equity threatens the firm's survival. Too much equity relative to debt reduces the return on the stockholders' investment.

What is the relationship between current assets and current liabilities? Current assets provide the funds necessary to meet current liabilities as they come due. But a business with a comfortable cushion of total current assets relative to its total current liabilities

Table 2-1

Financial Condition of the Sample Corporation
12/31/90 Balance Sheet

Cash	$ 50,000	
Accounts Receivable	175,000	
Inventory	150,000	
Total Current Assets		$375,000
Factory Building	$ 75,000	
Machinery and Equipment	50,000	
Total Fixed Assets		$125,000
Total Assets		$500,000
Accounts Payable	$100,000	
Note Payable	50,000	
Other Current Liabilities	25,000	
Total Current Liabilities		$175,000
Long-Term Liabilities		75,000
Total Liabilities		$250,000
Common Stock	$100,000	
Retained Earnings	150,000	
Total Stockholders' Equity		$250,000
Total Liabilities and Equity		$500,000

still may not escape financial problems. For example, a problem may exist when inventory and accounts receivable make up most of the current assets. A business can't pay an expense or retire a liability with either asset. Instead, it needs cash to meet its obligations. Even a profitable business can find itself short of that critical asset.

Using the analytic tools demonstrated throughout this book would indicate that the Sample Corporation is financially sound. The fundamental relationships apparent in the firm's financial image fall within the guidelines that define prudent financial management.

Importance of Balanced Accounts

One of the simplest accounting tenets remains one of the most important: A balance sheet must balance. A change in any asset, liability, or equity account effects a comparable change in other accounts that make up the balance sheet. No account can change independently.

For example, the decision to increase inventory requires a matching change elsewhere in a firm's financial structure. In some circumstances, a business will exchange cash for the inventory. One asset replaces another.

Often an increase in liabilities accompanies the initial increase in a firm's assets. The business employs trade credit—accounts payable or other borrowed funds—to finance the asset acquisition. Less frequently, an increase in stockholders' equity will provide the funds necessary to increase assets.

In any event, no balance-sheet account can change without a corresponding change in another balance-sheet account. Overlooking this relationship in the midst of all of the daily management decisions necessary to operate a business can lead to some serious financial problems.

That potential justifies recognition of that important accounting principle in:

FINANCIAL FACT 3:

A balance sheet must balance.

The total assets a business owns must equal the total claims on those assets. Almost every business decision affects that relationship. Consequently, that relationship should become a consideration in

Chapter 3

Evaluating a Firm's Financial Progress

A balance sheet projects an image of a firm's financial condition at a particular time. The most recent balance sheet actually summarizes the cumulative results of all of a firm's financial transactions since it initiated operations, but that balance sheet provides little information about recent financial progress. The prudent business manager complements any analysis of the balance sheet with a review of a firm's income statement.

An income statement measures the financial gain or loss generated by a business between two points. A typical income statement measures a firm's financial progress from the beginning to the end of a month, quarter, or year. An attentive financial manager measures the firm's gains or losses across all of those periods.

Bottom Line

An income statement matches the expenses incurred by a business during a specific period against its sales. The difference between the two measures the operating results for that period. To illustrate, assume the Sample Corporation generates $1 million in sales and incurs $950,000 in expenses for the twelve months ending 12/31/90. A simplified income statement measures the firm's operating results as:

Sales	$1,000,000
Expenses	(950,000)
Net income	$ 50,000

The bottom line of the income statement—the central concern for most business managers—isolates the Sample Corporation's $50,000 in profits for the year ending 12/31/90. That translates directly into a $50,000 increase in the stockholders' equity account on the firm's balance sheet. Of course, this simplified income statement provides little information that is useful for positive financial management. A more practical statement for management analysis and action categorizes a firm's expenses.

Expense Categories

A properly constructed income statement organizes the total expenses a business incurs during an operating period into three major categories:

1. Cost of goods sold

2. Operating expenses

3. Interest expenses

The cost-of-goods-sold total represents all of the expenses associated with the inventory actually sold during an operating period, including material purchase costs. However, a manufacturer would add in the labor and overhead expenses incurred in the production process.

Note that the cost of goods sold by a business seldom coincides with the cost of inventories purchased or produced during an operating period. Nor does that total match the cost of inventory on hand at the beginning or the end of the period covered by an income statement. However, an important relationship does exist between the cost-of-goods-sold total and the inventory on hand at the beginning—that purchased (or manufactured)—and at the end of an operating period:

	Beginning Inventory
Plus:	Additions to Inventory
Equals:	Total Inventory Available for Sale

Minus:	Ending Inventory
Equals:	Cost of Goods Sold

The total goods available for sale during an operating period include a firm's beginning inventory plus all additions made to inventory during the period. Subtracting the inventory on hand at the end of the operating period from that total identifies the cost of goods sold.

Most expenses, apart from those associated with the acquisition or manufacture of inventory, fit into the operating-expense category. These include the expenses that arise from marketing the firm's products, as well as the general and administrative expenses associated with operating a business.

Interest expenses stand apart from operating expenses, even though they can significantly affect the bottom line in a business. A unique characteristic makes them a separate category on an income statement. These expenses arise from the financial structure of the firm rather than directly from its operations. A financial structure without debt eliminates interest expenses, but a business always incurs operating expenses.

One cost incurred by a successful business does not fit into any of the three major expense categories. That's the income tax assessed against the firm's earnings. Since it doesn't qualify as an operational or financial expense, those taxes appear on an income statement as a separate deduction. Although income taxes may become significant in a profitable business, they stand apart from actual operating expenses.

Let's see how the major expense categories enter into the final construction of an income statement.

Reaching the Bottom Line

The bottom line of an income statement registers a firm's operating results, measuring the difference between total revenues and total expenses. However, simply comparing those two totals provides little useful information for positive financial management. Consequently, before reaching the bottom line, an income statement subtracts each category of expenses in turn from the total sales revenue. The amount remaining after each deduction provides a different perspective of a firm's operating results. The view at each step helps isolate the factors that determine earnings. Let's expand

19

the Sample Corporation's income statement for the year ending 12/31/90 to illustrate the financial views that develop as an income statement progresses from a firm's sales to its bottom line. That illustration begins by dividing the $950,000 in total costs incurred during that year into the appropriate categories:

1.	Cost of Goods Sold	$700,000
2.	Operating Expenses	205,000
3.	Interest Expenses	20,000
4.	Taxes	25,000
	Total Expenses	$950,000

Beginning with the Sample Corporation's $1,000,000 sales volume for the year ending 12/31/90, the income statement first subtracts the cost of goods sold to measure the firm's gross profit:

Sales	$1,000,000
Cost of Goods Sold	(700,000)
Gross Profit	$ 300,000

The gross profit measures the actual gains that proceed from sales. These gains represent the total margin available to cover operating expenses, as well as to provide any earnings the business might enjoy.

The income statement then subtracts the total operating expenses from the gross profits. This result identifies the firm's operating income. Some statements refer to that total as the earnings before interest and taxes, or EBIT. In the Sample Corporation's circumstance:

Gross Profit	$300,000
Operating Expenses	(205,000)
Operating Income (or EBIT)	$ 95,000

Operating income represents the *pure profits* a business generates. Pure profits stand apart from the financing costs and income tax assessments not directly related to operations. Relating those pure profits to total sales provides another important measure of a firm's operating efficiency.

The income statement then deducts any interest charges incurred from operating income. That measures the firm's earnings before taxes, or EBT. The Sample Corporation's income statement continues:

Operating Income	$95,000
Interest Charges	(20,000)
Earnings Before Taxes (EBT)	$75,000

The earnings-before-taxes total recognizes the effects of a firm's financial structure on its operating results. The larger the debt load, the more significant the effect. That should not imply that a business should avoid using debt, but any debt a business uses should contribute to an increase in operating income that exceeds its interest cost.

From another perspective, the earnings-before-taxes total provides an important indication of a firm's ability to absorb a financial setback. Any drop in gross profit or increase in expenses must exceed the earnings-before-taxes total in order to impose a loss on a business.

To complete the progression from the total sales to the bottom line, an income statement recognizes a firm's income-tax obligation. That assessment does not qualify as a business expense, since it contributes nothing to a firm's operations. Nevertheless, it does reduce the net earnings retained by a business. The income statement subtracts that obligation from the earnings before taxes to identify the firm's net income.

Completing the Sample Corporation's income statement:

Earnings Before Taxes	$75,000
Income Taxes	(25,000)
Net Income	$50,000

Net income represents the most important measure of a firm's operating results. Indeed, the bottom line stands as the final symbol of business success or failure.

But a business manager can't focus only on the bottom line. The net income actually represents a residual—what's left over from all the financial interrelationships associated with operating a business. Table 3-1 emphasizes their significance with the view of the Sample Corporation's complete income statement. That view isolates the major factors that determine the bottom-line results.

Table 3-1

The Sample Corporation Income Statement
(Year Ending 12/31/90)

Sales	$ 1,000,000
Cost of Goods Sold	700,000
Gross Profit	$ 300,000
Operating Expenses	205,000
Operating Income (EBIT)	95,000
Interest Charges	20,000
Earnings Before Taxes (EBT)	$ 75,000
Taxes	25,000
Net Income	$ 50,000

Incidentally, the distinction between a firm's before and after tax income does not affect the principles that orient most financial management decisions. Most of the discussion that follows recognizes a firm's potential income-tax obligations only when they enter into an actual decision process.

The information apparent in a business income statement calls for one major qualification. An income statement shows only the visible financial factors that determine a firm's net income. The financial manager also must recognize another perspective of business income—opportunity costs.

Opportunity Costs

The bottom line of an income statement registers the net profits a business produces. In any circumstance, profits represent financial progress and increase the stockholders' equity. However, to set the stage for later discussion, we should draw a distinction between the earnings recognized by an income statement and a firm's actual financial performance. Standing alone, the net profit that appears on an income statement does not adequately measure financial performance. A manager also should recognize the opportunity costs a business incurs.

In simple terms, an opportunity cost represents profits foregone. A firm that incurs opportunity costs earns less than it could. Indeed, foregone opportunity costs can make a profitable performance unsatisfactory.

In some instances, a manager can measure a firm's opportunity costs directly. For example, a business incurs an opportunity cost when it fails to take trade discounts its suppliers offer in exchange for early payment for purchases. Each discount lost represents earnings foregone.

To illustrate, assume a business buys $200,000 in material during the year from suppliers who allow a 2% discount for payment within ten days after each purchase. The business incurs $4,000 in opportunity costs ($200,000 x 2%) from the failure to take the discounts. In this instance, you can measure the opportunity costs directly.

But some opportunity costs a business incurs remain more elusive, subject only to indirect measurement or management estimates. For example, a business incurs an opportunity cost whenever it lacks the stock necessary to fill a customer's order. If the customer accepts later delivery, the firm's opportunity cost—the stock-out cost— remains limited to the administrative expense associated with a back order. However, if the customer decides to buy from a competitor, the opportunity cost becomes the potential profit on the lost sale.

If the inconvenience makes the customer shift all future purchases to competitors, the opportunity cost then becomes the potential profits on all those lost sales. Stock-out costs do not appear in an income statement, but they still damage a firm's earnings.

A business also incurs opportunity costs when it holds assets that exceed the level necessary for its operations. Should the business have to use borrowed funds to carry those assets, the opportunity costs appear in the form of higher interest expenses on the income statement. Eliminating the excess assets and associated interest costs can increase the firm's earnings.

Even in the absence of any debt, excess assets impose another, less apparent opportunity cost on a business. That comes from the income foregone on the funds invested in the excess assets. Thus, dollars invested in excess accounts receivable might increase the firm's earnings if converted into additional inventory. Alternatively, dollars invested in excess inventory might be profitably employed in fixed assets that will improve a firm's operating efficiency. From the most conservative viewpoint, eliminating any excess assets frees funds for investment in interest-bearing instruments that contribute to earnings.

Later discussion shows why effective control of the investment in assets should be a focal point for positive financial management. Here we only suggest that excess assets impose another opportunity cost on a business, either directly or indirectly. We emphasize that potential financial damage in:

FINANCIAL FACT 4:

Opportunity costs hurt earnings.

Opportunity costs do not appear as a separate expense category on the income statement, but they remain nonetheless real. Chapter 4 discusses the important distinction between the financial progress measured by an income statement and the actual cash flow in a business.

Accrual Accounting and Cash Flow

An income statement identifies the financial or accounting income a business generates. The bottom-line total translates directly into a corresponding change in the value represented by the stockholders' equity account on the balance sheet.

But accrual accounting underlies the construction of an income statement. That accounting process measures a firm's income by properly matching a firm's revenues and expenses within a particular accounting period. The sales total on an income statement *seldom matches* a firm's actual cash receipts during a particular operating period. Nor do the expenses duplicate its cash disbursements. The apparent discrepancy exists because accrual accounting recognizes sales and expenses when incurred by a business, regardless of when the associated cash transactions occur. So, the income a business generates does not necessarily match its cash flow.

Positive financial management requires a clear distinction between the information provided by the accrual accounting process and the actual cash flow through a business. This chapter illustrates that distinction.

Financial View

A comparative look at the distinction between the financial and cash flows in a business centers on the Beta Company, a small wholesale operation. During the year ending 12/31/90, Beta averaged $100,000 per month in sales. However, that sales volume left the firm with only break-even operating results. Beta's total expenses matched its total sales volume:

Sales	$100,000
Cost of Goods Sold	(70,000)
Operating Expenses	(30,000)
Net Earnings	—

The income statement suggests two important financial characteristics about Beta's operations.

First, the cost of goods sold averages 70% of sales. Whatever Beta's monthly sales volume, seventy cents of every dollar represents the firm's average cost for the items sold. Second, the $30,000 in operating expenses included on the income statement remains constant from month to month. This total represents the fixed expenses Beta incurs, regardless of its monthly sales volume, up to the limit set by the firm's present capacity. Recognizing that the monthly operating expenses remain constant, it seems that pushing Beta's monthly sales above the $100,000 mark will make the company profitable.

That happy circumstance developed during the early months of 1991. Beta continued its $100,000 monthly break-even performance in January. Then sales shot up to $125,000 in February and $150,000 in March. As the firm's monthly comparative income statements indicate, the sales spurt made Beta very profitable:

	January	February	March
Sales	$100,000	$125,000	$150,000
Cost of Goods Sold			
(70% of sales)	(70,000)	(87,500)	(105,000)
Operating Expenses	(30,000)	(30,000)	(30,000)
Net Earnings	—	$ 7,500	$ 15,000

The larger sales volume enabled Beta to accumulate $22,500 in total earnings during the first quarter of 1991. The total revenue for the quarter exceeded Beta's total expenses by that amount.

Unfortunately, the cash disbursements necessary to pay those expenses rose more rapidly than the cash collections that proceeded from the sales increase. The profitable growth spurt exhausted Beta's cash operating balance. The firm encountered a cash flow problem. The following section shows how that problem developed, despite the firm's profitable operations.

Cash View

The cash flow problem that accompanied Beta's sales increase developed inevitably from the pattern apparent in the firm's collection, purchase, and payment habits:

1. Beta collects 70% of the accounts receivable arising from each month's sales in the month immediately following; the payments for the remaining 30% of each month's volume comes in the second month following the sales.

2. Beta accurately anticipates each month's sales volume and purchases only the inventory necessary for that volume.

3. Beta respects the thirty-day trade credit terms suppliers allow for all purchases; consequently, cash payment for purchases actually occurs in the same month that Beta sells the inventory.

4. Beta pays all operating expenses in the same month incurred.

The cash flow that developed from Beta's collection and disbursement history was adequate for Beta's monthly $100,000 volume during 1990. At that volume, monthly cash collections matched monthly cash expenditures. Beta's $20,000 operating cash balance absorbed any temporary disruptions in the normal cash flow pattern.

The cash requirements set by Beta's rising sales volume in February and March quickly absorbed that $20,000 operating balance and forced the business into a deficit cash position. Table 4-1 illustrates the cash accounting process that traces the natural development of that problem. The table summarizes the Beta Company's actual cash receipts and expenditures for the first three months of 1991.

January's cash flow continues the convenient balance between receipts and expenditures set by the firm's break-even operations during 1990. Cash collections from November and December sales match the $100,000 in cash expenditures necessary to conduct January's business. Beta begins and ends the month with the same $20,000 cash balance.

Table 4-1

Beta Company
Cash Receipts and Expenditures
(1/1/91–3/31/91)

	January	February	March
Beginning Cash	$ 20,000	$ 20,000	$ 2,500
Collections:			
70% of Prior*			
Month's Sales	70,000	70,000	87,500
30% of Second*			
Month's Sales	30,000	30,000	30,000
Total Cash Available	$120,000	$120,000	$120,000
Disbursements:			
Purchases	$ 70,000	$ 87,500	$105,000
Operating Expenses	30,000	30,000	30,000
Ending Cash	$ 20,000	$ 2,500	($ 15,000)

*Assumes that Beta's monthly sales volume totaled $100,000 in both November and December of 1990.

The sales spurt in February upsets that balance. Beta begins that month with the same $20,000 balance left at the end of January. The firm then collects $100,000 in payments for sales generated during the previous two months. However the cash payments necessary for February's larger sales volume total $117,500. The $17,500 increase in expenditures comes from the higher costs necessary to generate that volume. Beta then ends February with only $2,500 in cash on hand, which becomes the beginning cash balance in March. It then collects $117,500 from sales made in January and February. Those collections plus the beginning balance provide the firm with $120,000 to meet March's cash expenditure requirements.

Unfortunately, Beta's March cash expenditure requirements total $135,000. The firm needs $105,000 to pay the inventory purchase costs that enter into that month's cost of goods sold, plus $30,000 to pay normal operating expenses. Those requirements leave Beta $15,000 short of the cash necessary to fund its operations in March. Indeed, as shown in Table 4-1, the firm presumably ends March with a $15,000 cash deficit.

Of course, no business can conduct operations with a real cash deficit. So, Beta filled the gap in its cash flow by temporarily deferring payment to some suppliers. That damaged the firm's credit rating, but it avoided the financial embarrassment that comes from bouncing checks.

Beta's experience illustrates that the financial flow measured by the accrual accounting process seldom corresponds directly to the actual cash flow in a business. Beta accrued $22,500 in profits during the first quarter of 1991, but it ended March with a $15,000 cash deficit. Add on the $20,000 in cash on hand at the beginning of the year and Beta's deficit cash flow during the first quarter actually totals $35,000. The potential for cash deficits makes understanding the distinction between the financial and cash flows in a business essential:

FINANCIAL FACT 5:

Cash flow seldom corresponds directly to financial flow in a business.

Cash flow and financial flow remain closely interrelated. Collections translate sales accrued as accounts receivable into cash. Similarly, cash retires the accounts payable that accrue from purchases made with trade credit. Every accrual accounting entry registers or anticipates a cash receipt or disbursement, but seldom do they all occur simultaneously.

Profits Versus Cash Flow

Another view of the Beta Company's circumstances helps clarify the distinction between accrued profits and cash flow. The balance sheets in Table 4-2 provide a comparative view of Beta's financial position at 12/31/90 and 3/31/91.

The financial image on the 12/31/90 balance sheet developed from Beta's $100,000 monthly break-even sales volume. The firm's $20,000 operating cash balance was noted previously. The $130,000 in accounts receivable includes $100,000 from December sales plus $30,000 still outstanding from November sales. The $70,000 inventory provides the stock necessary to satisfy January's sales volume.

The liability section of the 12/31/90 balance sheet includes the

29

Table 4-2

Beta Company
Comparative Balance Sheets

	12/31/90	3/31/91
Cash	$ 20,000	($ 15,000)
Accounts Receivable	130,000	187,500
Inventory	70,000	105,000
Total Assets	$220,000	$277,500
Accounts Payable	$ 70,000	$105,000
Bank Loan	50,000	50,000
Total Liabilities	$120,000	$155,000
Common Stock	$ 50,000	$ 50,000
Retained Earnings	50,000	72,500
Total Liabilities and Equity	$220,000	$277,500

$70,000 in accounts payable for the inventory purchased during December. Beta's creditors allow thirty days trade credit for purchases. So the cash payment for all of December's purchases comes due in January. Beta also has a $50,000 bank loan.

Finally, the stockholders' equity account at 12/31/90 totals $100,000. Half of that amount represents the stockholders' original investment. The other half accrued from earnings generated prior to 1990. The $100,000 total equity leaves Beta in reasonably sound financial shape. Coupled with Beta's liabilities, the equity provides the funds adequate for the level of operations that prevailed throughout 1990. However, the 3/31/91 balance sheet shows how Beta's profitable sales increase upset that relationship.

Note the $22,500 increase in retained earnings on the 3/31/91 balance sheet. This corresponds with Beta's first-quarter earnings. Each dollar in profit naturally increases the stockholders' equity account by a comparable amount. But that financial progress did not prevent Beta's $15,000 cash deficit at 3/31/91. In fact, the higher sales volume actually caused the problem. The deficit developed from the expansion in accounts receivable and inventory that proceeded naturally from the sales increase.

Thus Beta's accounts receivable at 3/31/91 totaled $187,500. That represents $150,000 created from March's sales, plus 30% (or $37,500) still uncollected from February's sales. More significantly, it represents a $57,500 increase over the total outstanding at 12/31/90. The firm's inventory also increased from $70,000 at 12/31/90 to $105,000 at 3/31/91. Beta anticipated another $150,000 sales volume in April 1991.

As Financial Fact No. 3 reminds us, a balance sheet must balance. The $92,500 incremental investment in accounts receivable and inventory cannot accrue independently. Those funds must flow from sources that register a corresponding cumulative change in Beta's other balance sheet accounts.

Another look at Table 4-2 indicates that a portion of the necessary funds came from a $35,000 increase in accounts payable from 12/31/90 to 3/31/91. (To help emphasize the point of the illustration, we disregard the deferred payments to suppliers that temporarily solved Beta's cash flow problem.) The increase in payables complements the increase in inventory necessary to accommodate April's projected $150,000 sales volume.

Beta's $22,500 increase in retained earnings also helps balance the increase in receivables and inventory. However, since the firm's bank loan remained constant, that exhausted the source of funds available from the bottom side of the balance sheet.

Beta's cash account provided the only other source for the remaining $35,000 necessary to match the increase in receivables and inventory. That absorbed the $20,000 operating balance held at 12/31/90 and left the firm with a $15,000 cash deficit. Of course, presuming that Beta continues the profitable $150,000 monthly sales volume, the hypothetical deficit will soon disappear. Profits originally accrued as a portion of a firm's receivables become cash when collected. But this should not obscure the point that accounting profits do not necessarily provide immediate cash benefits for a business. Business managers who overlook this may find their profitable operation running out of cash.

Need for Both Views

The accrual accounting process used to construct an income statement remains essential for financial management. The process operates on the premise that a business should recognize a sale when it occurs, regardless of when it receives cash payment for the sale. Accrual accounting also registers expenses as incurred, regardless of when the business actually remits payment. Properly matching sales and expenses stands as the only logical way to assess a firm's financial performance during any particular operating period.

The accrual accounting process also underlies the construction of a business balance sheet. Properly accruing, matching, and categorizing assets, liabilities, and equity enables a manager to properly evaluate a firm's financial position.

But the Beta Company's experience clearly illustrates that a financial manager also needs a clear perception of the cash flow process. A financial manager must anticipate the firm's required cash disbursements and project its cash receipts, and then must fill any void that develops when the disbursements outface the receipts. The failure to maintain the distinction between accrued sales or income and current cash receipts can lead to financial embarrassment.

Annual Cash Flow

The bottom line of an income statement provides the first estimate of a firm's financial progress. The second estimate adds any depreciation expenses to the earnings total to measure annual cash flow. This total identifies the net incremental cash generated from the firm's operations. The financial manager views the annual cash flow as funds available to retire debt, pay dividends, or increase assets.

The annual cash flow generated seldom appears as a clearly delineated increase in a firm's bank account. The daily fluctuations in a firm's cash receipts and disbursements obscure that total. In fact, many business managers find the concept itself somewhat questionable. While it is easy to accept income as a source of cash, some find it more difficult to understand how depreciation contributes to annual cash flow.

A look at the Common Company, a young service company, clarifies the concept. Common initiated operations with $150,000 in cash invested by its stockholders. The company employed $100,000 to purchase the equipment necessary for its operations. That left $50,000 as an operating cash balance and the following beginning balance sheet:

Cash		$ 50,000
Equipment (cost).	$100,000	
Less: Accumulated Depreciation	—	
Equipment (net)		100,000
Total Assets		$150,000
Stockholders' Equity		$150,000

During its first year in business, the Common Company generated $50,000 in earnings from $500,000 in sales. The firm's $450,000 in total expenses that year included $20,000 in depreciation. That reflected management's decision to employ straight-line depreciation for the five-year useful life anticipated from Common's equipment. Straight-line depreciation takes the depreciable cost of an asset and divides it by its useful life to determine the annual depreciation expense.

Common's management also made an important decision before initiating operations. Management decided to conduct business during the first year strictly on a cash basis. The firm paid cash for all purchases and operating expenses and received cash for all sales. That produced the following operating results:

Cash Sales	$500,000
Cash Expenses..	(430,000)
Depreciation...	(20,000)
Net income	$ 50,000

The income statement emphasizes that depreciation is a noncash expense for the Common Company. The firm paid cash for its equipment at the time purchased, but that actually represented an exchange of assets—$100,000 in cash for $100,000 in equipment. Subsequently, the depreciation expense that allocates the cost of the equipment over its life requires no cash outlay. So coupling that expense with income actually measures Common's annual cash flow from operations. Depreciation represents a source of cash for the business.

To prove that claim, look at Common's balance sheet at the end of its first year in business:

Cash		$120,000
Equipment (cost).	$100,000	
Less: Accumulated Depreciation	(20,000)	
Equipment (net)		80,000
Total Assets		$200,000
Stockholders' Equity		$200,000

The $50,000 increase in the stockholders' equity account over the stockholders' initial investment matches Common's $50,000 in earnings for the year. At the same time, the net value of the firm's equipment, $80,000, reflects the $20,000 depreciation charge against the historical cost.

Finally, observe the sources of the $120,000 held in Common's cash account at the end of its first year:

Cash from Original Investment	$ 50,000
Cash from Net Income	50,000
Cash from Depreciation	20,000
Cash per Balance Sheet	$120,000

Common's $20,000 noncash depreciation expense translates directly into a $20,000 increase in the firm's cash balance. In any circumstance, coupling that expense with net income measures the annual cash flow generated by a business. We emphasize this view of a firm's annual cash flow in:

FINANCIAL FACT 6:

Net income plus depreciation measures annual cash flow.

That total has important implications for both managers and creditors.

Chapter 5

The Foundation for Financial Analysis

The balance sheet and income statement provide the raw material for financial management. However, you must distill information from those statements to evaluate a firm's financial position and financial performance. The distilling process—financial analysis—uses a number of ratios and formulas to extract and interrelate the elements included in financial statements thereby identifying a firm's strengths and weaknesses. This chapter reviews the management logic and criteria that provide the foundation for effective financial analysis.

Sample Analysis

Another look at the Sample Corporation, focusing on the interrelationship between the firm's investment in inventory and its average sales volume, demonstrates how financial analysis can help increase earnings. Specifically, information from Sample's balance sheet (Table 2-1) and income statement (Table 3-1) helps to identify the average age of the firm's inventory.

The average age of the inventory a business owns tells us how many days a typical item remains in stock before being sold. A two-step calculation identifies that average:

1. Divide a firm's annual cost of goods sold by 360 to obtain the average daily cost of goods sold.

2. Divide the firm's current investment in inventory by the average daily cost-of-goods-sold total.

Table 3-1 showed that the Sample Corporation's cost of goods sold totaled $700,000 for the year ending 12/31/90. So, the first calculation becomes:

$$\text{Average Daily Cost of Goods Sold} = \frac{\$700,000}{360} = \$1,944$$

From Table 2-1, Sample's inventory at 12/31/90 totaled $150,000. To complete the calculation:

$$\text{Average Age of Inventory} = \frac{\$150,000}{\$\ 1,944} = 77 \text{ days}$$

At 12/31/90 the average inventory item remained in the Sample Corporation's stock for seventy-seven days. From another perspective, we can say that the company has inventory on hand to meet its normal sales requirements for that period.

To recognize how the Sample Corporation can use that information to increase its earning requires a look at the $50,000 bank note that appears on the 12/31/90 balance sheet. Previously, we surmised that those borrowed funds helped support Sample's investment in current assets. Here we will look at the $8,000 in interest the business paid on the note during 1990.

The basic accounting equation indicates that reducing the Sample Corporation's assets will eliminate the need for the support provided by the bank loan. The seventy-seven-day average inventory age suggests one potential approach.

Assume that most of the Sample Corporation's suppliers fill every order from the company within thirty days. In no circumstance does the company have to wait more than forty-five days for delivery. Certainly a business with such dependable suppliers does not need inventory on hand sufficient for seventy-seven days' sales. The Sample Corporation has excess stock at 12/31/90.

The firm can eliminate the overstock by deferring unnecessary purchases, thus reducing the average age of its inventory from seventy-seven to perhaps fifty days. Each day's reduction in the average age lowers the firm's inventory by $1,944. That simultaneously reduces the need for the bank loan by an equal amount.

The full twenty-seven-day reduction in the average age of the Sample Corporation's inventory reduces the firm's total assets by $52,488 ($1,944 x 27). That eliminates the need for the $50,000 bank loan and the associated $8,000 interest expense. At the same time, inventory sufficient for fifty days' sales leaves the Sample Corporation with a comfortable cushion against unforeseen delays in supplier deliveries. The firm has little risk of sustaining any stock-out costs.

The management perspective gained from a simple, two-step calculation process opens the door to higher profits for the Sample Corporation. But a complete analysis of the firm's financial circumstances might provide even more profitable opportunities.

Method and Meaning

The Sample Corporation's experience demonstrates the profit potential from financial analysis and illustrates the important distinction between calculation and interpretation—the difference between method and meaning.

Ratios and formulas summarize and quantify financial interrelationships. But no management magic rests on a financial ratio, nor does a financial formula conjure up any management sorcery. The results of any calculation merely provide another view of a firm's financial circumstances. That view becomes meaningful for management only when set within the context of a firm's unique circumstances.

Thus, for the Sample Corporation, the seventy-seven-day average age for inventory initially stands only as an isolated financial fact—how long the average inventory item remains in stock. This fact stands out only when we recognize the efficient service provided by the firm's suppliers. That made the profitable reduction in inventory feasible.

Alternatively, a business subject to erratic supplier shipping practices might find a seventy-seven-day average inventory age necessary to provide an adequate safety stock. (Safety stock represents that portion of a firm's inventory held to reduce or prevent stock-out costs.) A unique marketing strategy or an anticipated boost in sales also might encourage a business to carry more inventory than necessary when measured by normal standards. So financial ratios and formulas are used to initiate financial analysis, but management must supply the meaning that makes that analysis useful.

Analytic Criteria

Common sense remains an essential ingredient in financial analysis. But using some comparative analytic criteria significantly increases the benefits that develop from that management attribute.

Many ratios become meaningful only when placed against a bench mark or standard for comparison. You obtain those bench marks from three sources:

1. Traditional comparative criteria

2. Industry comparative criteria

3. Internal comparative criteria

Now, let's see how these comparative criteria contribute to positive financial management.

Traditional Comparative Criteria

Traditional rules of thumb provide some useful comparative financial management standards. For example, a two-to-one debt-to-equity ratio—a firm's total debt divided by its total equity—traditionally marks the maximum credit limit for a business. Creditors supply two dollars to that business for every dollar supplied by the owners. A higher ratio presumably makes a business financially unstable. The creditors' risk of not being repaid becomes too high. To avoid that risk, many creditors refuse to extend additional credit to a firm with a debt/equity ratio that exceeds the traditional two-to-one standard.

A two-to-one current ratio stands as another traditional mark of financial stability. That ratio—total current assets divided by total current liabilities—presumably provides a firm with the liquidity necessary to withstand an unforeseen business setback. As the current ratio falls below two-to-one, so does a firm's ability to absorb a financial reverse.

Of course, many financially sound businesses have debt/equity ratios that exceed the two-to-one traditional standard. Others function comfortably with current ratios that fall below two-to-one. But the standard ratios provide a bench mark for comparison.

Industry Comparative Criteria

The most sensible approach to informative financial analysis focuses on comparative ratios obtained from other firms in the same industry. This comparison provides valuable insight into the relative financial condition and performance of a firm. For example, a firm's two-to-one debt/equity ratio may satisfy the traditional guideline. But if the ratio stands well above the industry standard, the business may be operating at a disadvantage relative to its competitors. A significant difference suggests the need for further investigation.

Any comparative analysis should employ data from companies with similar operating characteristics. It makes little sense to compare a local firm with a $1 million annual sales volume to a national one generating $100 million in sales annually. Financial guidelines appropriate for one may be ill-suited for the other.

This creates a minor problem for the independent business manager, who usually finds the data for direct financial comparison unavailable from other firm's in the industry. Small, privately held businesses seldom release financial information to competitors. Fortunately, a business manager can obtain comparative standards indirectly from a number of sources.

The *Annual Statement Studies* prepared by Robert Morris Associates (RMA) provides perhaps the most useful general collection of comparative data for the independent business manager. This national association compiles financial statement data provided by its member bank-loan and credit officers.

Because RMA uses both total assets and annual sales volume to categorize comparative data, a business can obtain useful comparative financial criteria for its own circumstances. A small business need not employ comparative standards that are more suitable for larger businesses.

RMA also provides a composite common-size balance sheet and income statement for each category of business. A common-size income statement expressed each account as a percentage of total sales. A common-size balance sheet expressed each account as a percentage of total assets or total liabilities and stockholders' equity. These statements enable a business to compare its own common-size statements to those from its competitors.

Figure 5-1 provides a representative view showing these comparative criteria for manufacturer's of paint, varnish, lacquer, enamel and allied products. Note, in Figure 5-1 that RMA also provides three values for each ratio—the median, the upper quartile, and the lower

Fig. 5-1.   RMA Comparative Criteria

MANUFACTURERS - PAINT, VARNISH, LACQUER, ENAMEL & ALLIED PRODUCTS   SIC# 2851

	Comparative Historical Data			Current Data Sorted By Sales					
	6/30/87-3/31/88	6/30/88-3/31/89	6/30/89-3/31/90	0-1MM	1-3MM	3-5MM	5-10MM	10-25MM	25MM & OVER
					38(6/30-9/30/89)		76(10/1/89-3/31/90)		
Type of Statement									
Unqualified	41	33	43		2	4	6	11	20
Qualified	2	2	1					1	
Reviewed	38	36	30	1	8	8	7	5	1
Compiled	29	28	27	2	10	5	6	2	2
Other	21	16	13	1	4	2		4	2
	ALL 131	ALL 115	ALL 114	4	24	19	19	23	25
NUMBER OF STATEMENTS									
ASSETS	%	%	%	%	%	%	%	%	%
Cash & Equivalents	7.6	6.1	7.2		8.0	8.7	5.3	8.7	4.1
Trade Receivables - (net)	28.2	28.6	29.2		27.5	30.3	30.2	29.0	28.8
Inventory	28.5	32.5	29.2		31.0	36.7	34.4	33.0	29.4
All Other Current	2.4	2.4	1.3		.9	1.2	.8	.9	2.5
Total Current	66.7	69.6	69.8		67.3	76.9	70.8	71.7	64.9
Fixed Assets (net)	25.1	22.0	21.8		24.1	16.8	21.2	20.6	25.8
Intangibles (net)	1.3	1.7	2.1		3.3	.3	1.0	.7	2.7
All Other Non-Current	6.9	6.7	6.3		5.3	6.0	7.0	7.0	6.6
Total	100.0	100.0	100.0		100.0	100.0	100.0	100.0	100.0
LIABILITIES									
Notes Payable-Short Term	6.5	9.1	9.4		11.8	10.8	9.0	11.1	5.8
Cur. Mat.-L/T/D	4.1	2.6	2.7		2.5	2.4	2.6	3.3	2.4
Trade Payables	17.8	17.7	18.2		18.8	23.7	16.4	18.3	15.7
Income Taxes Payable	1.0	.6	.6		.4	.3	1.2	.3	.8
All Other Current	7.5	7.0	7.1		6.6	4.9	9.3	5.2	8.8
Total Current	37.0	37.0	37.9		40.0	42.0	38.5	38.2	33.6
Long Term Debt	16.8	15.6	13.9		13.5	8.3	16.2	15.8	15.0
Deferred Taxes	.6	.5	.6		.2	.1	.7	.5	1.6
All Other Non-Current	2.2	2.1	2.7		4.0	.5	.7	3.1	3.3
Net Worth	43.5	44.7	44.9		42.3	49.1	44.1	42.4	46.6
Total Liabilities & Net Worth	100.0	100.0	100.0		100.0	100.0	100.0	100.0	100.0
INCOME DATA									
Net Sales	100.0	100.0	100.0		100.0	100.0	100.0	100.0	100.0
Gross Profit	33.6	33.2	33.1		35.4	29.3	34.2	30.9	32.1
Operating Expenses	28.7	29.2	29.0		31.7	27.0	30.7	25.9	26.7
Operating Profit	4.9	4.0	4.1		3.7	2.3	3.5	5.0	5.4
All Other Expenses (net)	.9	.9	.9		1.0	.7	.7	1.3	.9
Profit Before Taxes	4.0	3.1	3.2		2.7	1.7	2.8	3.6	4.5
RATIOS									
Current	2.8	3.2	2.8		3.7	3.0	2.1	2.9	2.7
	1.9	1.9	2.0		1.9	1.8	1.6	2.2	2.1
	1.3	1.4	1.3		1.1	1.3	1.4	1.3	1.5
Quick	1.4	1.6	1.5		1.9	1.7	1.2	1.9	1.3
	1.0	.9	.9		.8	.9	.8	1.3	1.1
	.7	.6	.7		.6	.6	.7	.7	.9

Ratio	Comparative Historical Data						Current Data Sorted By Assets			
Sales/Receivables	10.5 8.3 6.6	10.0 8.1 6.3	9.9 8.3 6.7		33 38 57	11.0 9.6 6.4	10.6 8.7 7.5	8.7 8.0 7.1	10.1 8.9 6.8	8.8 7.3 6.2
(days)	35 44 55	37 45 58	37 44 54		41 65 94				41 50 59	
Cost of Sales/Inventory	8.3 5.5 4.0	6.6 4.8 3.5	6.6 4.9 3.5		8.8 5.6 3.9	6.3 5.0 3.8	6.3 4.9 3.6	7.1 4.8 3.6	6.2 4.8 4.0	
(days)	44 68 91	55 74 96	55 74 104		58 73 96	58 74 101	51 76 101	59 76 91		
Cost of Sales/Payables	14.1 9.1 6.7	13.1 9.6 6.6	13.1 9.8 6.9		13.4 9.4 6.0	20.7 7.4 6.2	16.5 10.7 7.2	16.2 10.6 5.8	12.0 10.0 8.8	
(days)	26 40 54	28 38 55	25 37 53		27 39 61	18 49 59	22 34 51	30 37 41		
Sales/Working Capital	5.0 8.1 16.0	4.8 7.5 13.8	5.3 7.1 14.2		5.2 7.0 39.4	4.7 7.9 14.5	5.9 8.8 13.5	4.7 6.5 19.2	5.4 6.5 10.4	
EBIT/Interest	(117) 10.2 3.8 2.0	(94) 6.7 2.9 1.0	(103) 8.3 3.4 .7		(20) 5.4 2.2 .3	(15) 9.7 3.8 .5	9.6 2.0 .3	(22) 10.2 4.2 1.2	5.6 2.8 1.2	9.5 4.1 .8
Net Profit + Depr., Dep. Amort./Cur. Mat. L/T/D	(83) 8.4 2.6 1.6	(64) 7.0 3.3 1.3	(70) 6.7 4.1 1.1		(14) 4.6 3.4 .8	(10) 10.2 5.0 -.2	(11) 4.2 1.2	(15) 6.0 2.9 .5	(19) 12.2 5.2 2.1	
Fixed/Worth	.3 .6 1.1	.2 .5 .9	.2 .5 .9		.2 .6 1.7	.2 .3 .4	.3 .5 .6	.2 .4 1.9	.3 .6 .9	
Debt/Worth	.7 1.4 3.0	.6 1.3 2.8	.7 1.2 2.6		.7 1.4 4.7	.5 1.1 2.2	.9 1.3 2.3	.6 1.4 5.2	.7 1.1 2.7	
% Profit Before Taxes/Tangible Net Worth	(126) 35.6 21.0 10.5	(110) 24.4 12.0 2.1	(110) 31.3 12.6 1.1		(21) 32.1 6.4 -6.6	24.0 12.2 -5.7	33.6 12.1 -5.5	(22) 44.9 18.5 6.2	33.2 19.1 2.1	
% Profit Before Taxes/Total Assets	14.9 8.6 4.3	10.6 5.8 .5	13.5 6.3 -.1		10.3 4.9 -2.6	9.6 5.6 -2.7	17.4 5.8 -2.4	14.5 7.9 1.0	16.3 8.8 -.2	
Sales/Net Fixed Assets	20.2 10.3 6.0	26.4 11.5 7.2	27.2 11.9 7.3		24.1 10.9 7.0	28.1 19.9 10.6	27.6 16.6 5.9	30.8 12.3 9.8	11.7 8.6 5.6	
Sales/Total Assets	2.9 2.3 1.9	2.8 2.3 1.9	2.9 2.4 2.0		3.0 2.5 2.1	3.0 2.7 2.1	2.9 2.4 2.0	2.9 2.3 2.0	2.5 2.0 1.8	
% Depr., Dep. Amort./Sales	(113) 1.2 1.6 2.8	(103) 1.0 1.6 2.4	(108) 1.0 1.5 2.3		(21) 1.1 1.8 2.4	(18) .9 1.3 1.9	1.2 1.5 2.3	2.9 2.3 2.5	.3 1.0 1.3	(24) 1.3 1.8 2.2
% Officers' Comp/Sales	(43) 2.6 4.2 6.3	(39) 1.8 3.4 5.2	(39) 2.7 4.1 6.9		(10) 2.7 4.7 8.4	2.5 3.9 7.3	2.5 3.4 4.7			
Net Sales ($)	2052588M	1820431M	4176717M		3336M	49089M	74170M	138568M	379041M	3534513M
Total Assets ($)	1005539M	856706M	2268041M		1553M	22622M	30454M	55877M	271876M	1885859M

M = $thousand   MM = $million

Reprinted with permission, copyright Robert Morris Associates 1990

41

Interpretation of Statement Studies Figures

RMA recommends that Statement Studies data be regarded only as general guidelines and not as absolute industry norms. There are several reasons why the data may not be fully representative of a given industry:

(1) The financial statements used in the *Statement Studies* are not selected by any random or statistically reliable method. RMA member banks voluntarily submit the raw data they have available each year, with these being the only constraints: (a) The fiscal year-ends of the companies reported may not be from April 1 through June 29, and (b) their total assets must be less than $250 million.

(2) Many companies have varied product lines; however, the *Statement Studies* categorize them by their primary product Standard Industrial Classification (SIC) number only.

(3) Some of our industry samples are rather small in relation to the total number of firms in a given industry. A relatively small sample can increase the chances that some of our composites do not fully represent an industry.

(4) There is the chance that an extreme statement can be present in a sample, causing a disproportionate influence on the industry composite. This is particularly true in a relatively small sample.

(5) Companies within the same industry may differ in their method of operations which in turn can directly influence their financial statements. Since they are included in our sample, too, these statements can significantly affect our composite calculations.

(6) Other considerations that can result in variations among different companies engaged in the same general line of business are different labor markets; geographical location; different accounting methods; quality of products handled; sources and methods of financing; and terms of sale.

For these reasons, RMA does not recommend the Statement Studies *figures be considered as absolute norms for a given industry. Rather the figures should be used only as general guidelines and in addition to the other methods of financial analysis. RMA makes no claim as to the representativeness of the figures printed in this book.*

Fig. 5-1. RMA Comparative Criteria (cont.)

quartile. The median figure falls in the middle when RMA ranks the ratios for all the firm's within a specific size category. The upper quartile represents the figure halfway between the median and the highest values. The figure halfway between the median and the lowest ratio becomes the lower quartile. By providing three values for each ratio, RMA enables business managers to compare their firms with the "average" firm, as well as with the typical business in the top and bottom halves of each category.

The median ratio, or middle value among all firms included in the survey, provides a convenient standard for comparative financial analysis. For example, assume a paint manufacturer with a $1.5 million average sales volume has a two-to-one debt/equity ratio. The RMA median ratio stands at 1:4. The firm's two-to-one ratio exceeds the comparative standard. Its debt load exceeds the statistical average.

A business may justify a higher debt/equity ratio. But a significant deviation from the norm deserves explanation. Failure to find that explanation should encourage the business to reduce its debt. Otherwise, the firm will operate at a comparative financial disadvantage.

From another perspective, RMA's upper and lower quartile ratios set reasonable financial limits for a business. For example, reviewing the same $1mm-$3mm sales category in Figure 5-1, note the 4.7 debt/equity ratio registered by the lower-quartile business. The firm's relative debt burden is higher than that carried by almost 75% of the other businesses in the same category. Perhaps a business can justify a debt/equity ratio that exceeds the industry norm, but exceeding the limit set by the lower-quartile firm inevitably risks financial instability.

On the other hand, the upper-quartile firm's .7 debt/equity ratio marks a practical lower limit on the debt that a paint manufacturer should use. That a lower debt limit exists may come as a surprise to many conservative business managers. However, the business that uses little or no debt usually generates a below-average return on its stockholders' equity.

Internal Comparative Criteria
Internal comparative analysis focuses on changes apparent in a firm's financial circumstances across successive operating periods.

The analysis isolates any unfavorable trends that might call for management action. Internal comparative analysis commonly takes two forms.

One form employs the same financial data a business develops for external comparative analysis. But internal comparative analysis places the ratios in a sequence that matches the order of the firm's operating periods. That helps the perceptive analyst identify developing trends that deserve management attention.

For example, assume that the comparative debt/equity ratio for a business over four successive operating periods appears as:

Operating Period	1	2	3	4
D/E Ratio	1:6	1:8	2:0	2:2

The comparative view indicates a growing debt burden on the business. That implies a weakening financial condition. At the same time, external comparative analysis may show that even the 2.2 ratio rests well within industry standards. Nevertheless, the trend deserves management attention.

The other form of internal comparative analysis employs common-size financial statements. Common-size statements merely restate the accounts that make up a firm's income statement as a percentage of total sales. A comparative look at common-size income statements provides a more detailed perspective than a manager gains from ratio analysis alone.

Table 5-1 shows the common size income statements for the Window Manufacturing Company. Comparative analysis then attempts to isolate trends, either favorable or unfavorable, suggested by changes in any expense category relative to sales.

Note the comparative common-size income statements for Window Manufacturing Company. The declining net profit as a percentage of sales certainly represents an unfavorable trend. At the same time, we can see that the decline stems primarily from the firm's rising cost of goods sold. That cost has risen from 62% of Window Manufacturing's sales in 1988 to 64% in 1990.

The comparison in Table 5-1 includes the underlying accounts that make up Window Manufacturing's cost of goods sold. This allows a

Table 5-1

Window Manufacturing Company
Comparative Common-Size Income Statements

	1988	**1989**	**1990**
Sales	100.0%	100.0%	100.0%
Cost of Goods Sold	62.0	62.9	64.0
Materials	31.4	32.1	32.9
Labor	15.0	15.9	18.0
Overhead	15.6	14.9	13.2
Gross Profit	38.0	37.1	36.0
Operating Expenses	30.4	32.1	29.8
Selling	10.0	11.2	9.0
General	15.1	15.1	15.1
Administrative	5.3	5.9	5.7
Operating Profit	7.6	5.0	4.8
Interest	.5	1.0	1.1
Profit Before Taxes	7.1	4.0	3.7
Taxes	2.3	1.3	1.2
Net Profit	4.8	2.8	2.5

better view of the expense categories that deserve management attention. In this instance, rising material and labor costs relative to sales stand as the financial culprits.

More detailed common-size income statements often include every significant expense category. That helps identify financial trends that summary accounting totals may obscure. For example, assume that a firm's material costs relative to sales increase by 5%, while its overhead costs decline by the same relative amount. The firm's relative cost-of-goods-sold total remains the same. The business manager who fails to look beyond the latter relationship allows a favorable financial trend to mask an unfavorable one. Over all, the business is no worse off than before, but the potential for improvement exists. Common-size income statements fill a natural void left by traditional financial analysis and make a valuable contribution to positive financial management.

Of course, the focus of any aspect of financial analysis centers on comparative analysis:

Comparative criteria provide the foundation for financial analysis.

In the absence of the appropriate comparative data, many financial ratios and formulas lose much of their potential management value. Before discussing those formulas and ratios, let's review the unique conceptual approach to financial analysis offered here.

Perspectives for Management

Financial ratios and formulas stand as essential management tools. This book shows how those tools can contribute to positive financial management in a business enterprise. That approach focuses on:

1. Performance analysis

2. Component analysis

3. Structural analysis

Competent financial management requires a look at a firm's financial circumstances from all three perspectives.

Performance Analysis

Performance analysis begins with a look at the operating results in a business—the bottom line of the income statement. But any analysis that stops at the bottom line does not provide an adequate assessment of a firm's performance. To emphasize that, we separate performance analysis into two phases.

The first phase applies the basic analytic yardsticks to the income statement to analyze a firm's profit performance. That analysis does concentrate on the bottom line, but other measures of profit performance are also important.

You can't evaluate a firm's net profits properly without also looking at its operating profits. A large interest burden can make net profits unsatisfactory, while operating profits may meet industry standards. Nor can conclusions be drawn from looking at operating profits without also examining gross profits. Below-average operating expenses can conceal a gross profit margin that falls below industry standards. Indeed, analyzing profit performance requires evaluation of every level of a firm's operating results.

The second phase of performance analysis evaluates management. Indeed, a satisfactory profit performance does not necessarily represent a satisfactory management performance. A business that appears to do well might do better.

An evaluation of management's performance relies primarily on two key financial ratios. One ratio measures the return a business earns on its stockholders' equity. The other gauges how efficiently management employs the assets. Both help distinguish management performance from profit performance.

Component Analysis

Component analysis focuses on each of a firm's major asset accounts as a separate profit center. That presumes that better inventory management can improve earnings, even though sales remain constant. The same benefit accrues from more efficient accounts receivable and fixed-asset management. In fact, the premise that justifies component analysis suggests that increasing sales is not the only way to improve a firm's operating performance.

Practical limits exist on how efficiently a business can manage its assets. Reducing inventory too much can seriously damage sales. Excessive credit restrictions can drive perspective customers to competitors. Certainly, financial trade-offs exist. Nevertheless, the information derived from component analysis makes a valuable contribution to positive financial management.

Structural Analysis

Structural analysis examines the more important interrelationships among the financial elements that make up a firm's balance sheet, as well as the interrelationship among those elements and the income statement. After all, the most efficient asset management does not preclude financial problems for the business with an unbalanced financial structure.

Structural analysis concentrates on two specific characteristics of a firm's financial position, liquidity and leverage. Liquidity measures provide estimates of a firm's ability to meet its obligations promptly. Sensible liquidity management becomes a logical complement to sensible component management. Leverage analysis focuses on the debt load in a business. Excessive debt creates an unbalanced financial structure and raises the potential for serious financial problems.

In any event, no aspect of financial analysis stands alone. No analytic perspective provides all of the answers necessary to orient sensible financial management decisions. Positive financial management results by using the whole analytic package.

Section 2

Performance Analysis

Chapter 6

Analyzing Profit Performance

Evaluating profit performance is a logical starting point for financial analysis. However, you can draw few conclusions directly from dollar profit figures. Knowing that a firm's net income after taxes totals $100,000 doesn't tell us whether that performance is good or bad. The figure becomes important only when we measure those results as a percentage of the firm's total sales. Moreover, a complete evaluation requires a look at all four perspectives of the profits generated by a business:

1. Gross profit margin

2. Operating profit margin

3. Pretax profit margin

4. Net profit margin

Table 6-1 presents the comparative income statements that summarize the financial progress by the Galvez Manufacturing Company during the years ending 12/31/89 and 12/31/90. Galvez manufactures paint products, so we can also incorporate the RMA comparative data from Figure 5-1 into the discussion.

Gross Profit Margin

The difference between the total sales during an operating period and the cost of the goods sold measures a firm's gross profits.

Table 6-1

Galvez Manufacturing Company
1989 and 1990 Income Statements

	1989	1990
Sales...	$1,035,000	$1,185,000
Cost of Goods Sold.......................	641,700	750,500
Gross Profit.................................	$ 393,300	$ 434,500
Operating Expenses	325,300	361,200
Operating Income (EBIT).................	$ 68,000	$ 73,300
Interest Expenses.........................	10,200	13,100
Earnings Before Taxes (EBT)...........	$ 57,800	$ 60,200
Taxes*	11,590	12,310
Net Income	$ 46,210	$ 47,890

*Federal and State Income Taxes

Relating that difference to the sales total provides the first measure of a firm's profit performance:

$$\text{Gross Profit Margin} = \frac{\text{Sales - Cost of Goods Sold}}{\text{Sales}}$$

Note that the gross profits can be substituted directly from the income statement for the numerator in the calculation. However, the approach here isolates the two major factors that interrelate to produce the gross profits in a business.

The equation for the Galvez Company's 1990 income statement becomes:

$$\text{Gross Profit Margin} = \frac{\$1,185,000 - \$750,500}{\$1,185,000}$$

$$\text{Gross Profit Margin} = \frac{\$ 434,500}{\$1,185,000} = 36.7\%$$

The average Galvez Company sales dollar contributed almost thirty-seven cents to the firm's total gross profits in 1990. The following section reviews the management implications that arise from the financial interrelationships that produced this margin.

Analyzing the Gross Profit Margin

The gross profit margin in a business develops from the interrelationship between a firm's price structure and its purchase and production costs. An inadequate gross profit margin implies that a firm's product costs are too high or its prices too low. In this instance, the data in Figure 5-1 show that the Galvez Company's gross profit margin compares favorably with the 35.4% industry standard for similar firms.

The evaluation of the gross profit margin also should include a look at any variation in that margin across successive operating periods. Using the same calculation process, we find that the Galvez Company generated a 38% gross profit margin in 1989. So the 1990 margin actually represents a 1.3% drop from the previous year. Despite the company's comparative edge over the industry standard, that decrease deserves explanation. That explanation can be found by comparing the percentage increase in sales in 1990 with the percentage rise in the firm's cost of goods sold (CGS). The comparative percentage develops from the calculations:

$$\frac{\% \text{ Increase}}{\text{in Sales}} = \frac{1990 \text{ Sales} - 1989 \text{ Sales}}{1989 \text{ sales}}$$

$$\frac{\% \text{ Increase}}{\text{in Sales}} = \frac{\$1,185,000 - \$1,035,000}{\$1,035,000} = 14.5\%$$

Then, repeating the calculation for the cost of goods sold totals:

$$\frac{\% \text{ Increase}}{\text{in Sales}} = \frac{1990 \text{ CGS} - 1989 \text{ CGS}}{1989 \text{ CGS}}$$

$$\frac{\% \text{ Increase}}{\text{in Sales}} = \frac{\$750,500 - \$641,700}{\$641,700} = 17.0\%$$

The Galvez Company's product costs rose 2.5% more rapidly than the firm's prices in 1990. That naturally results in a smaller gross profit margin.

Of course, we lack the information necessary to identify the actual financial culprit here. The problem might stem from inadequate cost controls, or the company might need to pass inflationary increases in product costs onto its customers by pushing up its sales prices. But the analysis provides a view of a potential problem that deserves management attention.

Operating Profit Margin

A firm's operating expenses include all of the costs incurred from normal operations, apart from those associated with the cost of good sold. Deducting those expenses from gross profits measures the firm's operating profits. Relating those profits to total sales enables us to evaluate the performance measured by the gains from the firm's overall operations. The calculation becomes:

$$\text{Operating Profit Margin} = \frac{\text{Operating Profits (EBIT)}}{\text{Sales}}$$

The Galvez Company's operating profit for 1990 is:

$$\text{Operating Profit Margin} = \frac{\$ \ 73,300}{\$1,185,000} = 6.2\%$$

The company's operations produced 6.2 cents in profits from each sales dollar in 1990. Let's see how that serves as a gauge of the firm's operating effectiveness.

Analyzing the Operating Profit Margin

Operating expenses do not include the cost of any borrowed funds or income taxes. Consequently, the operating profit margin becomes the best measure of a firm's ability to produce any financial gains.

Another glance at Figure 5-1 indicates that the Galvez Company's 6.2% operating profit margin stands far above the 3.7% average among comparable firms in its industry. The company's competitors apparently operate less efficiently. However, a better view of a firm's operating results can be obtained by interrelating the operating profit margin with the gross profit margin. After all, a firm's operating profits follow deductions for both the cost of goods sold and operating costs. Effective cost control in one area can disguise ineffective cost control in another, even though the operating profit margin appears satisfactory.

The Galvez Company's 36.7% gross profit margin in 1990 stood above the 35.4% average for comparable firms. So, the firm's above average operating results suggests that the firm has managed to operate efficiently while also holding product costs under control. Logically, the positive results become complementary. This merely emphasizes that management cannot rely on efficient product cost control alone to preserve its operating profit margin. Effective operating cost control also remains essential.

The operating profit margin provides the best measure of a firm's overall profit performance. But a firm's financing decisions also have a significant impact on the final earnings total the business finally realizes. The pretax profit margin registers that impact.

Pretax Profit Margin

Borrowed funds enter into the financial structure of almost every business enterprise, but the interest charges for those funds stand apart from a firm's product costs and operating expenses. To identify earnings before taxes (EBT), an income statement deducts interest charges from the operating profits. Relating the remainder to total sales identifies the pretax profit margin:

$$\text{Pretax Profit Margin} = \frac{\text{Earnings Before Taxes}}{\text{Sales}}$$

In the Galvez Company's circumstance, the pretax profit margin in 1990 becomes:

$$\text{Pretax Profit Margin} = \frac{\$\ \ \ 60,200}{\$1,185,000} = 5.1\%$$

The Galvez Company's financing charges lowered the firm's pretax profit margin to 5.1% of its sales. Since a business seldom has significant influence on the income taxes extracted from its earnings, the pretax profit margin provides perhaps the best measure of a firm's actual earnings.

Analyzing the Pretax Profit Margin

A firm's financial structure has a significant influence on its profit performance. The more debt a business employs, the larger that influence becomes. However, the fact that interest charges reduce the pretax earnings total on an income statement does not imply that a business should avoid using borrowed funds. Indeed, a business easily can justify the interest charges that proceed from the proper use of debt.

That holds true when an increase in operating profits develops from borrowed funds and exceeds the accompanying interest charges. Borrowed funds also can increase the proportionate return a business provides to its stockholders. That potential exists even though using equity in place of debt might increase the firm's earnings total.

Figure 5-1 shows that the Galvez Company's 5.1% pretax profit margin stands well above the 2.7% industry standard. We previously noted that the Galvez Company operating profit margin stood above the industry standard. So the firm's interest charges apparently aren't damaging its profit performance, presuming that the borrowed funds are used to contribute to earnings.

We should recognize the signal that indicates excessive interest charges. It appears when those charges translate a satisfactory operating profit margin into an unsatisfactory pretax profit margin. Further analysis may justify that circumstance over a short-term period. But allowing excessive debt to erode a firm's earnings over a longer term doesn't make good business sense.

Net Profit Margin

Net profits represent the final measure of a firm's financial performance after recognizing its income tax obligation. The net profit margin evaluates the firm's overall ability to squeeze profits from each sales dollar. A manager identifies that figure in a similar way to the other profit margin calculations:

$$\text{Net Profit Margin} = \frac{\text{Net Profits}}{\text{Sales}}$$

The Galvez Company's net profit margin in 1990 appears as:

$$\text{Net Profit Margin} = \frac{\$\ \ 47,890}{\$1,185,000} = 4.0\%$$

Four cents out of each Galvez Company sales dollar finally reached the firm's bottom line.

Analyzing the Net Profit Performance

Expanding the net profit margin stands as a primary business objective. But standing alone, the net profit margin provides little useful information for management. Solving any mystery about a firm's net profit performance requires a look at the factors that determine the other three profit margins. In fact, the RMA industry data in Figure 5-1 does not include comparative net profit margin figures because the tax system often affects businesses unevenly. That makes net profit margins less reliable standards for comparison. The omission reminds us that any management analysis of a firm's profit performance must proceed beyond the obvious measure of its net profit margin. That warrants recognition in:

FINANCIAL FACT 8:

Analyzing a firm's profit performance requires a look at all four views of its profit margins.

From a different perspective, the failure to look at all four views of the profit margins a business produces sacrifices some of a firm's potential.

Chapter 7

Analyzing Management Performance

A satisfactory profit performance does not prove that a business enjoys effective management. A business with inept management may generate good profit margins simply because it has the right product in the right market at the right time. Evaluating management performance requires a look beyond a firm's profit margins and toward two interrelated performance gauges.

One gauge relates a firm's net profits to the accounting value of its stockholders' equity. That measures the proportionate return those profits provide to each equity dollar. Naturally, a better management performance produces a higher return on the stockholders' equity, or return on equity (ROE). However, even a poorly managed business that suffers from a below-average profit performance can generate an above-average ROE. That potential exists since borrowed funds can magnify the returns a firm's profits represent to its stockholders. That effect also can benefit the stockholders in a well-managed business. But the potential for a distorting influence from borrowed funds makes the ROE calculation a less reliable gauge of management performance.

The second gauge, the return on investment (ROI) calculation, reduces that distorting influence. The ROI calculation relates a firm's earnings to the total assets the business uses to generate those earnings. Usually, a higher ROI represents a better management performance.

Moreover, a direct relationship exists between the ROI in a business and the return on its equity. A higher ROI translates directly into a higher ROE. That suggests that ROI should become a focal point of positive financial management.

Return on Investment (ROI) and Return on Equity (ROE)

Table 7-1 presents the comparative balance sheets for the Galvez Manufacturing Company at 12/31/89 and 12/31/90. Subsequent analysis of those financial statements will raise some questions about the firm's financial circumstances. However, only two aspects of the statements become relevant here. That includes those elements that enter into the calculations that identify the firm's return on equity (ROE) and return on investment (ROI).

Table 7-1

Galvez Manufacturing Company
Comparative Balance Sheets

	12/31/89	**12/31/90**
Cash	$ 25,000	$ 10,000
Accounts Receivable	205,000	265,000
Inventory	352,500	335,000
Fixed Assets (net of depreciation)	50,000	105,000
Other Assets	15,000	20,000
Total Assets	$647,500	$735,000
Accounts Payable	$272,400	$241,000
Notes Payable (current).	75,000	150,000
Accrued Liabilities	13,500	19,510
Total Current Liabilities	$360,900	$410,510
Notes Payable (long-term)	40,000	30,000
Total Liabilities	$400,900	$440,510
Common Stock	100,000	100,000
Retained Earnings	146,600	194,490
Total Liabilities and Net Worth	$647,500	$735,000

The Galvez Company's assets totaled $647,500 and $735,000 on 12/31/89 and 12/31/90, respectively. The stockholders' equity amounted to $246,600 on 12/31/89 and $294,490 on 12/31/90. Those totals represent the accounting measure of the stockholders' interest in the firm's assets. Let's see how these items enter into the evaluation of management performance.

Calculating ROE

The income statement measures the profits a business generates for its stockholders. However, stockholders should view those profits from the investor's perspective and focus on the return those profits represent relative to the equity funds committed to the enterprise. That perspective develops from the calculation:

$$\text{ROE} = \frac{\text{Net Profits}}{\text{Stockholders' Equity}}$$

The stockholders' equity in the Galvez Company totaled $246,600 on 12/31/89. This includes the stockholders' initial investment, as well as all of the previous earnings retained in the business. The return on that equity provided by the company's $47,890 in net profits in 1990 comes from the calculation:

$$\text{ROE} = \frac{\$\,47,890}{\$246,600} = 19.4\%$$

The company's earnings in 1990 represent a 19.4 cent return for each equity dollar invested on 12/31/89. In the absence of any dividend payments, that translates into a 19.4% increase in the accounting value of the stockholders' equity.

Before examining ROE as a gauge of management performance, we first should eliminate a potential source of confusion associated with the ROE calculation process. That centers on the denominator in the ROE calculation. The example above uses the stockholders' equity as it stands at the beginning of the business year. While that may appear obvious, some analysts use the year-end equity total as the denominator. That naturally includes a firm's earnings for the year. Others use an average equity total, since earnings accrue incrementally throughout the year.

However, both of the latter methods distort a straightforward perspective of the return a firm's earnings represent for its stockholders. Using the equity total as it stands at the beginning of the business year provides a more consistent criterion for evaluating management's performance.

Analyzing ROE

The stockholders in any business expect a yield from their investment. The ROE calculation measures the yield a firm's earnings represent relative to the accounting value of the investment. From an investor's perspective, that return is more important than a firm's net profit margin. Moreover, ROE also becomes an important standard for evaluating management's performance.

Analyzing ROE seldom stands as a straightforward task. The analysis should begin with a look at comparative industry standards (not included in the RMA data in Figure 5-1). But in this instance, those standards may not provide reliable comparative criteria. A comparatively low ROE does not prove that a business suffers from inept management. Nor is a high ROE irrefutable evidence that a business enjoys effective management. In any circumstance, the evaluation process must recognize the interrelationship between a firm's financial structure and the return it generates on the stockholders' equity.

To demonstrate that interrelationship, let's compare two businesses that generate $200,000 in operating profits (EBIT). Both businesses employ $600,000 in total assets. But they have different financial structures. One business employs no debt, while the other uses $300,000 in borrowed funds. The comparative financial structures stand as:

	Firm 1	Firm 2
Total Assets	$600,000	$600,000
Total Liabilities	—	300,000
Stockholders' Equity	600,000	300,000
Liabilities and Equity	$600,000	$600,000

Firm 2 pays a 12% annual interest charge for its borrowed funds. Consequently, we can complete the comparative earnings and ROE totals for the two firms:

	Firm 1	Firm 2
Operating Profits (EBIT)	$200,000	$200,000
Interest Expenses	—	(36,000)
Profits Before Taxes	$200,000	$164,000
Taxes (30% average rate)	(60,000)	(49,200)
Net Profits	$140,000	$114,800
Return on Equity (ROE)	23.3%	38.3%

The absence of debt allows Firm 1 to register higher net profits. Yet the stockholders in Firm 2 enjoy a significantly higher return on their equity. That provides an important view of the positive contribution debt can make to a business. It also demonstrates that the return a business generates on its stockholders' equity cannot stand alone as a gauge of management performance. Indeed, management can use debt to magnify a modest profit performance into a ROE total that stands well above any comparative standard.

Generating a higher return on the stockholders' equity always remains a desirable objective. Within realistic limits, using debt to achieve that objective represents a reasonable management practice. But that practice also can create a distorted measure of management's performance. Nevertheless, the ROE calculation is a valuable device for evaluating management:

FINANCIAL FACT 9:

The ROE calculation measures the yield that a firm's earnings represent for its stockholders.

A satisfactory profit performance that leaves stockholders with a low return on their equity should raise a question about management's overall performance. In the absence of any other standard, stockholders should compare a firm's ROE to the yield available from alternative investment opportunities. That comparison may provide a better criterion for gauging management performance than the prevailing industry standard. In any event, the return on investment criterion provides an even better perspective of management performance.

Calculating ROI

The net profit margin measures the average return a business earns from each sales dollar. The ROE calculation identifies the yield the firm's cumulative earnings represent for its stockholders. But neither calculation measures how effectively management employs the dollars invested in a firm's assets. The ROI calculation gauges that effectiveness with the following calculation:

$$ROI = \frac{\text{Net Profits}}{\text{Total Assets}}$$

Let's use that calculation to assess how efficiently the Galvez Company's management used the firm's assets in 1990:

$$ROI = \frac{\$\ 47,890}{\$735,000} = 6.5\%$$

The Galvez Company's earnings represent a 6.5% return from each dollar invested in the firm's assets. Remember that the debt employed in the company's financial structure magnified that ROI into a 19.4% return on the stockholders' equity. However, the ROI calculation ignores that debt, except for the reduction in profits that develop from the interest charges. By relating net profits directly to the total assets available to generate a return, the ROI calculation provides a better measure of management's actual operating effectiveness. In fact, the interrelationships that determine the ROI in a business encompass almost every aspect of its operations.

An alternative approach to calculating the ROI a business produces ignores the impact interest costs and income taxes have on a firm's profits. That calculation relates a firm's operating profits to its total assets:

$$\frac{\text{Operating Return}}{\text{on Investment}} = \frac{\text{Operating Profit (EBIT)}}{\text{Total Assets}}$$

Remember that interest charges and income taxes do not result directly from a firm's operations, so this calculation provides an undistorted measure of management's operating effectiveness. Of course, management also influences the interest costs and income taxes a business incurs. Consequently, relating net profits to total assets provides a better perspective of management performance and a better criterion for orienting positive financial management.

Analyzing ROI

The assets a business owns represent an investment, regardless of the mixture of debt and equity that provides the funds invested in those assets. Those assets should generate a large enough return to justify continuing the investment. Should the return on that investment fall too low, the funds should be invested elsewhere.

That should make the return a business generates from its assets a major management concern. That suggestion proceeds from the premise that the financial interrelationships that determine a firm's ROI remain subject to direct management influence. The ROI calculation provides a summary view of management's impact on those relationships. Another look at the calculation emphasizes that fact.

The numerator in the ROI calculation represents the net profit margin held in each sales dollar. Holding a firm's total assets constant, any management effort that expands that margin translates into a higher return on that investment. For example, assume a business presently employs $500,000 in assets to generate a $1 million annual sales volume. A 5% net profit margin produces $50,000 in earnings and a 10% return on investment ($50,000/ $500,000). Any management action that expands the size of that profit margin will increase the firm's earnings. That increase also will produce a higher ROI for the business. Thus a 10% profit margin will push up the firm's earnings to $100,000 and raise its ROI to 20% ($100,000/$500,000).

Alternatively, the denominator in the ROI calculation registers management's ability to use a firm's assets efficiently. Using those assets more efficiently enables a business to conduct any specific sales volume with a smaller dollar investment. Holding the profit margin in those sales constant, this again creates a higher ROI for the business.

To illustrate, assume that the Galvez Company's initial 5% profit margin isn't subject to expansion. Perhaps competitive pressure precludes any sales price hikes, while inflationary pressure prevents any reduction in expenses. Nevertheless, more efficient asset management can still increase the firm's ROI.

That occurs if attentive management effort enables the firm to generate the same $1 million sales volume with only $250,000 in total assets. The $50,000 in net profits then represents a 20% ROI for the business ($50,000/$250,000).

That shows that a firm's ROI is not a function of profits alone. Instead, ROI directly reflects management's ability to generate profits while also employing the firm's assets efficiently. The conscientious business manager cannot ignore either without jeopardizing the firm's ROI.

A critical distinction enters into ROI analysis. Any increase in earnings that develops from a higher sales volume does not automatically translate into a better return from the firm's asset investment. That benefit develops only when the business achieves the sales increase without a concomitant expansion in assets. Indeed, sales volume becomes, at least conceptually, a less significant concern in positive financial management. Instead, as shown in Figure 7-1, that effort focuses on the ROI that develops from the interrelationship between a firm's profit margin and the asset investment used to generate that margin.

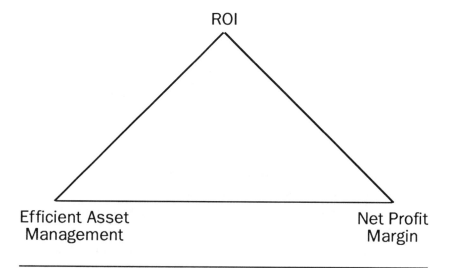

Fig. 7-1. The focal point for positive financial management.

By any standard, the Galvez Company's 6.5% ROI in 1990 represents an inadequate yield from the firm's assets. We noted in chapter 6 that the company's overall profit performance exceeded the comparative industry standards. So the substandard return on the firm's investment apparently results primarily from poor asset-management practices. The company's ROI in 1989 makes that conclusion even more disturbing. Management generated only a 7.1% return from the firm's asset investment during that year. The poor management performance in 1990 apparently represents an unsatisfactory norm. That emphasizes that a satisfactory profit performance does not necessarily reflect an effective overall management performance.

How ROI Affects ROE

Stockholders enjoy a higher yield on their equity whenever better management increases the firm's ROI. Alternatively, that yield falls whenever less effective management allows a drop in the return from the firm's total asset investment. A look at a business with an uncomplicated financial structure clarifies that direct relationship. The business doesn't use any debt. The stockholders' equity provides all of the financial support for the firm's $250,000 in assets. That makes a summary view of the firm's balance sheet appear as:

Total Assets	$250,000
Stockholders' Equity	$250,000

If management employs the firm's assets as efficiently as possible, any change in the return the business generates from those assets can develop only from a change in the earnings management extracts from sales. Note what happens as management expands the average profit margin held in each sales dollar:

Total Earnings	$25,000	$50,000	$75,000
ROI	10%	20%	30%
ROE	10%	20%	30%

Any increase or decrease in the return generated from assets creates a concurrent increase or decrease in the return on equity. This relationship exists in any business circumstance. Holding a firm's assets constant, any increase in earnings increases a firm's ROI. And that translates directly into a higher ROE.

Now, let's use the same business to show how effective asset management influences a firm's ROI and ROE. That calls for a departure from business reality. That departure assumes that the stockholders' equity changes in line with any increase or decrease in the total assets a business uses. Presumably, the stockholders contribute the additional equity necessary to support any increase in the firm's assets. Alternatively, the business refunds a portion of stockholders' equity whenever better management reduces the total asset investment necessary to conduct the firm's operations.

Assume that the firm's earnings will stand at $75,000, regardless of the size of that investment. As management employs the firm's assets more efficiently, we find:

Total Assets	$250,000	200,000	150,000
Stockholders' Equity	$250,000	200,000	150,000
Earnings	$ 75,000	75,000	75,000
ROI	30%	37.5%	50%
ROE	30%	37.5%	50%

Since the firm lacks any debt in its financial structure, the ROI equals the ROE. More significantly, both returns increase as management employs the firm's assets more efficiently. Of course in the real business world, more efficient asset management seldom results in any equity refund to shareholders. Instead, it enables a business to generate a larger sales volume from any fixed investment in assets. However, the beneficial effect on the firm's ROI and ROE remains the same.

Note that using debt in a firm's financial structure does not change the direct relationship. However, debt magnifies the change in the return on the stockholders' equity that develops from any increase or decrease in the return from a firm's total asset investment.

To demonstrate that effect, let's include some debt in the financial structure of this hypothetical business. Assume that the business supports its $250,000 asset investment with equal proportions of debt and equity.

The firm's simplified balance sheet becomes:

Total Assets	$250,000
Total Liabilities	$125,000
Stockholders' Equity	$125,000
Liabilities and Equity	$250,000

Assuming that more efficient asset management isn't possible, let's see what happens as wider profit margins raise the firm's earnings:

Earnings	$25,000	$50,000	75,000
ROI	10%	20%	30%
ROE	20%	40%	60%

This confirms that debt does not alter the direct relationship between the ROI and ROE. Moreover, using debt to finance 50% of a firm's assets doubles the impact any change in the ROI has on the ROE. Using larger proportions of debt magnifies that impact even more. From the other perspective, the effect decreases as debt occupies a smaller proportion of a firm's financial structure.

Note that to simplify the discussion we did not attribute any direct cost to the debt. Presumably we can ignore that cost since we use net earnings after interest and taxes in the return calculations. At the same time, the cost of borrowing naturally enters into any decision to use debt in a firm's financial structure. Here we emphasize the benefits stockholders enjoy whenever a business generates a higher return from its assets. The business manager who recognizes those benefits will remember:

FINANCIAL FACT 10:

Return on investment provides the focal point for positive financial management.

ROI stands as the most important criterion for evaluating management performance. It reflects management's ability to generate profits while using the firm's assets efficiently.

Section 3

Component Analysis

Chapter 8

Investment in
Accounts Receivable

Manufacturers and wholesalers sell merchandise in exchange for their customers' promise to pay later, rather than for cash. The accounting process marks those promises as accounts receivable. The accumulated receivables outstanding at any time typically represent a significant proportion of the total dollars invested in a firm's assets. This chapter reviews the factors that determine the size of that investment.

Formulas for Analysis

Regardless of sales volume, a smaller total asset investment can improve the ROI in a business. Ideally, a business should sell only for cash. That would eliminate the need for any investment in accounts receivable. But few businesses have that option. Requiring cash payment for all purchases eliminates many prospective customers who expect credit consideration. It limits sales, reduces profits, and lowers the return a business can generate from its assets.

The decision to extend credit consideration and carry the resulting investment in accounts receivables focuses on a trade-off. The trade-off compares the cost of carrying the investment in accounts receivable against the benefits that develop from a larger sales volume. The contribution to a firm's ROI that develops from the incremental sales must exceed the incremental costs associated with a larger investment in accounts receivable.

The same trade-off exists whenever a business considers a change in the factors that determine the investment in accounts receivable, regardless of the level of sales. Any change in those factors will induce a simultaneous, if not proportionate, increase or decrease in the firm's sales and receivables. Anticipating the impact on ROI becomes a necessary precedent to any management decision affecting the size of a firm's investment in accounts receivable.

Any analysis of that impact begins with a measure of a firm's investment in accounts receivable. Two calculations measure that investment:

1. Accounts-receivable turnover rate

2. Average collection period

Both calculations relate the size of a firm's investment in accounts receivable to its total sales volume. A smaller investment relative to a particular sales volume produces a better yield from a firm's assets.

Accounts Receivable Turnover Rate

The accounts-receivable turnover rate calculation gauges how often a business recycles each dollar invested in its accounts receivable over the course of the year:

$$\frac{\text{Accounts-Receivable}}{\text{Turnover Rate}} = \frac{\text{Annual Sales}}{\text{Accounts Receivable}}$$

Relating the Galvez Company's $265,000 investment in accounts receivable on 12/31/90 to its $1,185,000 sales volume for that year, we find:

$$\frac{\text{Accounts Receivable}}{\text{Turnover Rate}} = \frac{\$1,185,000}{\$\ 265,000} = 4.5$$

The Galvez Company collected and reinvested each dollar included in its receivables 4.5 times during 1990. From Figure 5-1, we find that the comparative industry average accounts receivable turnover rate stands at 9.6 times per year.

Since the Galvez Company's turnover rate is well below that standard, the firm apparently has an excess investment in accounts receivable. This partially explains the poor average yield from the firm's asset investment identified in chapter 7. Indeed, the potential reduction in accounts receivable from a higher turnover rate can improve the Galvez Company's ROI.

At any sales level, a higher turnover rate shrinks a firm's investment in accounts receivable and improves the average yield from its assets. A simple illustration, showing an abbreviated view of the MBA Company's financial structure, demonstrates those facts:

Accounts Receivable	$300,000
Other Assets	300,000
Total Assets	$600,000
Stockholders' Equity	$600,000

During the upcoming year, management expects to produce $90,000 in earnings from the MBA Company's projected $1,200,000 sales volume. That earnings total will produce a 15% yield from the firm's total asset investment ($90,000/$600,000). Of course, MBA's management explored the potential for increasing that yield.

Any increase in the MBA Company's projected sales or profits appears doubtful. Consequently, management focused on the potential benefits that could be derived from using its assets more efficiently. Among other possibilities, it projected the increase in MBA's ROI that would develop from more rapid accounts receivable turnover rates.

Since the MBA Company doesn't employ any debt, the funds released by reducing MBA's receivable investment presumably would flow directly to the stockholders as an equity refund. This remains an artificial assumption, but it helps clarify the direct relationship between the accounts-receivable turnover rate and the return a business generates from its assets. Table 8-1 demonstrates that relationship.

MBA management's analysis recognized that the firm presently turns its accounts receivable four times in the course of a year ($1,200,000/4 = $300,000). With $300,000 in other assets, that turnover rate leaves the MBA Company with the 15% return on its total asset investment. The following calculation identifies the impact

Table 8-1

Annual Turnover Rate	Investment in Accounts Receivable	Total Assets	ROI
4	$300,000	$600,000	15.0%
5	240,000	540,000	16.7%
6	200,000	500,000	18.0%
7	171,428	471,428	19.9%
8	150,000	450,000	20.0%

that higher turnover rates will have on MBA's investment in receivables:

$$\text{Investment in Accounts Receivable} = \frac{\text{Projected Sales}}{\text{Projected Turnover Rate}}$$

Increasing MBA's turnover rate from four to five times per year will reduce the firm's investment in accounts receivable to the $240,000 total in Table 8-1:

$$\text{Investment in Accounts Receivable} = \frac{\$1,200,000}{5} = \$240,000$$

Naturally, any drop in accounts receivable reduces the asset total that enters into the denominator of the ROI calculation. This increases the ROI for a business, whatever the level of earnings.

The final step in the analytic process relates the MBA Company's $90,000 in earnings to the shrinking asset totals in Table 8-1. Management can increase MBA's ROI to 16.7% by increasing the accounts-receivable turnover rate from four to five times per year. Accelerating that rate up to eight times per year will produce a 20% return from the firm's remaining asset base. Recycling the dollars invested in the firm's receivables even more rapidly will push that yield still higher.

Although there are limits on how rapidly a business can turn its investment in accounts receivable, the MBA Company's circumstances demonstrate the potential benefits a business can obtain by employing the dollars invested in its accounts receivable more efficiently.

Average Collection Period

The collection period calculation measures how long a firm's average sales dollar remains as an accounts receivable. A longer average collection period creates a larger investment in accounts receivable. One approach to identifying a firm's average collection period proceeds as:

$$\text{Average Collection Period} = \frac{360}{\text{Accounts-Receivable Turnover Rate}}$$

Using the Galvez Company's annual turnover rate calculated previously, we find:

$$\text{Average Collection Period} = \frac{360}{4.5} = 80 \text{ days}$$

The average Galvez Company sales dollar remains outstanding as an account receivable for eighty days. That collection period far exceeds the forty-two-day industry standard in Figure 5-1. That supports the suggestion that an excess investment in accounts receivable earns part of the blame for the firm's low ROI.

A useful alternative approach to calculating the average collection period proceeds in two steps:

1. Divide annual sales by 360 to determine the average daily sales volume,

2. Divide the accounts receivable total by the average daily sales volume to identify the average collection period.

Using the data from the Galvez Company to illustrate the calculation process.

$$1. \quad \frac{\text{Average Daily}}{\text{Sales Volume}} = \frac{\$1,185,000}{360} = \$3,292$$

$$2. \quad \frac{\text{Average Collection}}{\text{Period}} = \frac{\$265,000}{\$\ \ 3,292} = 80 \text{ Days}$$

This agrees with the average collection period identified above.

This average collection period calculation can be particularly useful for a firm whose sales occur seasonally. In that case, the most recent quarter's sales should be used in place of annual volume in the calculation process. For example, assume a business with a $1.2 million annual sales volume presently has a $250,000 investment in receivables. Based on the annual volume, either calculation process will show that the business has a seventy-five-day average collection period. However, in this instance, we find that $700,000 of the $1.2 million annual sales volume occurs in the final three months of the year. So a more realistic measure of the firm's average collection period focuses on that quarter's sales:

$$\text{Average Daily Sales Volume} = \frac{\$700,000}{90} = \$7,778$$

$$\text{Average Collection Period} = \frac{\$250,000}{\$\ 7,778} = 32 \text{ Days}$$

Thus, the apparent excess investment in receivables actually reflects the seasonal characteristics of the firm's sales. That provides a more realistic accounts receivable management perspective.

Conceptually, the turnover rate and collection period calculations provide the same information. A business with an excess investment in accounts receivable will have both a low turnover rate and a lengthy average collection period. As the business increases its accounts receivable turnover rate, its average collection period naturally shrinks. However, the collection period calculation provides a more useful perspective for managing a firm's investment in accounts receivable. A business manager can more easily relate that perspective directly to the credit and collection policies that determine the length of the firm's average collection period. In addition, the average collection period provides a better view of the increase or decrease in receivables that management should anticipate from any change in those policies.

Perspectives for Accounts Receivable Management

The average daily sales volume a business generates naturally affects the size of its investment in accounts receivable. A larger sales volume creates a larger investment. However, holding any daily sales volume constant, the size of that investment becomes directly attributable to the length of a firm's average collection period. The calculation that defines that relationship appears as:

$$\text{Average Daily Sales Volume} \times \text{Average Collection Period} = \text{Investment in Accounts Receivable}$$

To illustrate, a business with a $2,500 daily sales volume and a fifty-day average collection period will develop a $125,000 investment in accounts receivable: $2,500 x 50 = $125,000.

This direct relationship clarifies the conceptual link between a firm's credit and collection policies and the size of its investment in accounts receivable. The relationship emphasizes that a business can reduce its investment in receivables by implementing more stringent policies that shorten its average collection period. For example, assume that more stringent credit and collection policies reduce the above firm's average collection period to forty days. Presuming that the $2,500 daily sales volume remains constant, the firm's investment in accounts receivables will drop to $100,000 ($2,500 x 40).

Alternatively, the lengthier average collection period that develops from more liberal credit and collection policies will expand a firm's investment in accounts receivable. Assume that such policies extend the firm's average collection period to sixty days. Presuming that the $2,500 average daily volume remains unchanged, the firm's investment in accounts receivable rises to $150,000 ($2,500 x 60).

We can use the accounts receivable turnover rate calculation to illustrate the same relationship. However, the management implications that arise from that relationship become more apparent when we focus on the average collection period. Another look at Table 8-1 helps emphasize that fact. A more rapid accounts receivable turnover rate reduces a firm's investment in accounts and increases its ROI. But the potential for actually accelerating MBA's accounts receivable turnover rate remains unclear. The task may be relatively simple, or it may represent a formidable management challenge.

The potential for reducing the MBA Company's investment in receivables becomes more apparent when comparative average collection periods are included in the analysis. Using the different levels of accounts receivable in Table 8-1 we find:

Investment in Accounts Receivable	Average Collection Period (days)
$300,000	90
240,000	72
200,000	60
171,428	51
150,000	45

Now we see that the MBA Company's present investment in accounts receivable results from a ninety day average collection period. That far exceeds almost every industry norm. Consequently, any management effort to implement more stringent credit and collection policies should bring about a significant reduction in the firm's investment in accounts receivable.

The turnover rate calculation remains a useful gauge of management efficiency, but the discussion here demonstrates:

FINANCIAL FACT 11:

The average collection period provides the best perspective for managing a firm's investment in accounts receivable.

This will become more apparent in chapter 9, where we review alternative approaches to accounts receivable management that increase a firm's ROI. But first, let's examine the critical role accounts receivable play as a source of cash.

Contribution to Cash Flow

Customer payments on account, rather than sales, represent the primary source of cash for a business. So a better cash flow develops whenever a business manages the dollars invested in its accounts receivable more efficiently. And a shorter average collection period means a better cash flow.

Assume that a profitable business presently generates a $3,000 daily sales volume. Unfortunately, a sixty-day average collection period leaves the firm with a tight cash flow. Extracting the cash and accounts receivable accounts from the firm's most recent balance sheet highlights the problem:

Cash...	$ 3,000
Accounts Receivable	$180,000

Certainly, a $3,000 cash operating balance is inadequate for any business generating a $90,000 monthly sales volume. The firm has little defense against any unforeseen financial setback.

The accelerated cash flow that develops from a shorter average collection period can cure the problem. For example, assume that a more conscientious collection effort reduces the firm's average collection period from sixty to forty-five days.

The cash and receivable accounts then appear as:

Cash...	$ 48,000
Accounts Receivable	$135,000

The fifteen-day reduction in the average collection period shrinks the firm's investment in accounts receivable by $45,000 ($3,000 x 15). But the more significant benefit from the shorter average collection period appears as a simultaneous $45,000 increase in the cash account. The business no longer suffers from a cash deficiency. More effective accounts-receivable management relieved the tight cash flow.

We summarize the relationship between a firm's investment in receivables and its cash flow in:

FINANCIAL FACT 12:

Accounts receivable represent the primary source of cash for a business.

A better cash flow develops whenever a business manages the dollars invested in its accounts receivable more efficiently. But a shorter average collection period may not offer the best approach to a higher return on a firm's total asset investment. A firm's credit and collection policies also affect its sales and earnings, and that makes accounts receivable management a more complex task than it first appears. Chapter 9 discusses the major considerations that enter into that task.

Management Analysis: Accounts Receivable

The management analysis of a firm's investment in accounts receivable helps determine the appropriate credit and collection policies for a business. More liberal policies help boost sales and earnings but raise the cost of carrying an investment in accounts receivable. Alternatively, more restrictive policies dampen sales and earnings but help hold down the cost of carrying that investment. This chapter reviews the basic techniques for evaluating those trade-offs.

Credit Terms

A business establishes credit terms to limit the length of time a customer can defer payment for an open-account purchase. Inevitably, some customers ignore or overlook that limit, but the business' prompt payment habits contribute toward the general estimate of its creditworthiness. Most businesses try to pay within the terms set by suppliers. As a logical result, credit terms exert a significant influence on the length of a firm's average collection period and the size of its investment in accounts receivable.

Credit terms also influence the size of a firm's sales volume. Longer terms help increase that volume; shorter terms discourage sales. In any circumstance, managers should recognize how a firm's credit terms influence both its sales volume and the size of its investment in accounts receivable.

The Phoenix Company's experience illustrates the management analysis of a firm's credit terms. Phoenix operates in a highly competitive market. No company in its market enjoys a competitive advantage from product, price, or service differentials. However, research indicates that the company can gain a competitive advantage by extending credit terms that exceed the industry's present thirty-day norm. Consequently, management explored the gains from that potential advantage.

The evaluation process began with a review of the relevant aspects of the Phoenix Company's present operations:

1. The firm currently generates a $90,000 average monthly sales volume.

2. All customers observe the established thirty-day credit terms; that leaves the company with a $90,000 investment in accounts receivable.

3. The firm's total asset investment, including accounts receivable, averages $500,000.

4. Phoenix realizes a 5% net profit margin from its sales.

Market research indicates extending the Phoenix Company's credit terms by fifteen days will attract $20,000 in additional monthly sales, or a cumulative annual increase of $240,000. If the 5% net profit margin remains constant, the increase will push up the firm's annual earnings by $12,000. The research also indicates that each additional fifteen day extension in credit terms will have the same incremental effects on the company's sales and earnings.

The additional sales attracted by the longer credit terms also will increase the company's investment in accounts receivable. And that increase will exceed the rise in the monthly sales volume, since the company must extend the longer credit terms to all customers, the old as well as the new. Obviously, the analysis of the benefits anticipated from the extended credit terms cannot stop at the bottom line of the income statement. Instead, the analysis should focus on the impact the longer credit terms will have on the average return from the company's total asset investment. Table 9-1 illustrates one approach to that analysis.

Note that a $75,000 increase in accounts receivable (and total assets) will accompany the $20,000 sales increase anticipated from forty-

Table 9-1

Credit Terms and ROI
The Phoenix Company

Credit Terms (days)	Monthly Sales	Investment in Accounts Receivable	Annual Earnings	Total Assets	Return on Investment (ROI)
30	$ 90,000	90,000	54,000	500,000	10.8%
45	110,000	165,000	66,000	575,000	11.5%
60	130,000	260,000	78,000	670,000	11.6%
75	150,000	375,000	90,000	785,000	11.5%
90	170,000	510,000	102,000	920,000	11.1%

five-day credit terms. That expansion must occur since the firm's average collection period will match the longer credit terms. Extending the Phoenix Company's credit terms to sixty days will push sales up to $130,000 and the investment in accounts receivable up to $260,000. The longer selling terms will allow the average sales dollar to remain in the form of an account receivable for two months.

Table 9-1 also provides a view of the annual earnings and ROI the Phoenix Company can expect from the alternative credit terms. As noted above, each incremental $240,000 annual sales increase produces a $12,000 hike in earnings. Standing alone, that criterion suggests that the Phoenix Company should extend the longest credits terms possible.

However, the ROI criterion actually provides a better perspective for management. Another look at Table 9-1 indicates that extending the forty-five-day credit terms will raise the Phoenix Company's ROI from 10.8% to 11.5%. The higher earnings from the incremental sales easily compensate for the burden imposed by the larger investment in accounts receivable.

Extending the Phoenix Company's credit terms to sixty days provides another boost in the firm's ROI to 11.6%. However, the analysis indicates that extending credit terms beyond the sixty day term actually will lead to a lower ROI for the business. Terms beyond that limit create an increase in receivables that overburden the benefits from the incremental earnings. Extending sixty day credit terms seems the best option for the Phoenix Company. Of course, error exists in any such analysis. From a practical perspective, the forty-five-day credit terms probably become most appropriate.

This discussion simplifies the Phoenix Company's circumstances to help illustrate the analysis. Some complicating factors place a tighter limit on the benefits a business can obtain from offering longer credit terms.

First, we presumed that all of the company's customers pay according to the stated credit terms. However, some inevitably will take longer to pay. That will diminish the benefits projected from the longer credit terms.

Second, we assumed that the projected sales hikes would not affect any of the company's assets, other than the accounts receivable. Yet an increase in sales usually requires a proportionate increase in the size of a firm's investment in inventory. A rise in sales also may call for an increase in other assets, such as operating cash and prepaid expenses. So limiting the analysis to the expansion in accounts receivable overstates the benefits the business can expect from the longer selling terms.

Realistically, the sales attracted by the Phoenix Company's longer credit terms will come at the expense of the firm's competitors. Logically, those competitors will quickly match those credit terms offered by the Phoenix Company. That will leave the firm with the same sales volume, but with longer credit terms and a larger investment in accounts receivable. A temporary increase in the firm's ROI eventually may develop into a permanent reduction.

Finally, some of the new customers attracted by the Phoenix Company's longer credit terms will become additions to the firm's bad debt expenses. The longer a customer has to pay for a product, the greater the probability that he or she will lose the capacity to pay.

Despite these qualifications, the Phoenix Company's analysis emphasizes:

FINANCIAL FACT 13:

A change in credit terms can increase the return a business earns from its total asset investment.

Measuring the relationship between credit terms and ROI becomes more complex when those terms allow cash discounts if a customer pays for purchases early. The following section brings discounts into the analysis.

Cash Discounts

Many businesses set credit terms that authorize cash discounts in exchange for early customer payments. For example, 2% 10, Net 30 Day credit terms mean that a customer gains a 2% discount off the list purchase price if he remits payment within ten days. Otherwise, the seller expects full payment in thirty days.

Cash discounts presumably benefit both parties in the transaction. The buyer reduces his purchase costs when he takes the discount. The seller enjoys a better cash flow and a lower investment in accounts receivable. However, before introducing discounts into your credit terms, you should recognize how such allowances affect your earnings and ROI.

Returning to the Phoenix Company, let's assume that the competitive environment precludes any increase in the firm's present $90,000 monthly sales volume. Instead, management explored the prospects for improving the company's ROI by adding discounts to the existing thirty-day credit terms.

Research shows that half of the firm's customers will take advantage of a 1% cash discount allowed in exchange for payment within ten days. However, every customer will take a 2% discount allowed for early payment. Table 9-2 demonstrates how those payment habits will affect the Phoenix Company's operating results.

Naturally, any discounts a business allows shrink its profit margin. In the Phoenix Company's case, either of the proposed credit terms will reduce the company's earnings. The business manager who focuses on ROI doesn't make the bottom line of the income statement the sole management concern. A lower earnings total can be justified if a concurrent reduction in assets creates a higher ROI.

For the Phoenix Company, the reduction in assets anticipated from the proposed credit terms isn't adequate to provide a higher ROI. In fact, the 1% 10, net 30-day credit terms will lower the firm's ROI from 10.8% to 10.3%. Allowing 2% discounts for payments in ten days will reduce the company's ROI to 7.4%. Based on the summary

Table 9-2
Cash Discounts and ROI
The Phoenix Company

Credit Terms (days)	% Taking Discounts	Discounts Allowed (annual)	Net Earnings	Investment in Receivables	Total Assets	Return on Investment (ROI)
30	—	—	$54,000	90,000	500,000	10.8%
1% 10, net 30	50.0%	$ 5,400	48,600	60,000	470,000	10.3%
2% 10, net 30	100.0%	21,600	32,400	30,000	440,000	7.4%

analysis in Table 9-2, the firm should maintain its existing net thirty-day credit terms without allowing any cash discounts for early payment.

Additional analysis might justify adding the 1% discount for early payment to the Phoenix Company's credit terms. That potential exists if the cash released by the reduction in receivables can be reemployed in other assets that help increase the firm's earnings. But that potential seldom is large enough to justify allowing 2% cash discounts for early payments.

Don't presume that the results of the analysis illustrated in Table 9-2 will always preclude cash discounts from a firm's credit terms. While the analytic format doesn't change, the results may vary. Some businesses will find that allowing a reasonable discount for early customer payments helps increase the average return from their assets.

Financial View of Trade Discounts

A 2% discount for early payment obviously would be irresistible to the Phoenix Company's customers. But only half of the same customers will take advantage of a 1% discount allowed for payments made ten days after a purchase. Yet both discounts reduce a firm's net purchase costs. Recognizing the financial view of cash discounts explains that apparent contradiction.

A foregone discount really represents an interest charge a business pays for borrowed funds. When an option exists, the decision to take or skip a cash discount should focus on the annualized cost of those funds. Figure 9-1 illustrates this premise with a look at a $1,000 purchase made on 2% 10, Net 30 Day credit terms.

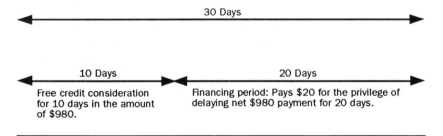

Fig. 9-1. A financial view of trade discounts. Assume a $1,000 purchase on 2% 10, net 30-day credit terms.

During the first ten days of the credit period, the purchaser enjoys the free use of $980 in credit consideration—the amount of the net, discounted purchase price. However, if he fails to pay by the tenth day, he pays the full $1,000 list price for the purchase. We can view the $20 difference between the discounted and the full list price as an interest charge the purchaser pays for using the initial $980 in credit consideration for an additional twenty days. That twenty-day term marks the length of the financing period, presuming the purchaser observes the upper limit set by the seller's credit terms.

Of course, to complete the financial view, we should translate the cost of the foregone discount into an annualized interest rate. The cost of missing a $10 or $20 discount may not appear significant. Yet many business managers overlook the fact that such discounts represent the cost of the seller's credit consideration for a relatively short period of time. The proper management perspective develops only when you annualize the interest cost.

One approach to that perspective begins by determining the total number of financing periods that accumulate from a firm's credit terms during a standard 360 day business year. Referring to Figure 9-1, the seller's 20 day financing period occurs eighteen times over the course of a year (360/20). The approximate, annualized interest rate appears when you multiply the number of credit periods in a year by the percentage cost of skipping a single discount.

For example, the business that foregoes a 1% discount allowed for payment in ten days pays an annualized 18% interest rate for the privilege of using the full 30 day credit period. Since that rate doesn't appear particularly high, it explains why only half of the Phoenix Company's customers will make the effort to take a 1% discount allowed for payment in ten days.

However, the same calculation process indicates that a business that foregoes a 2% discount pays a 36% annualized interest rate for the same credit consideration for the same term. Since almost every business manager will find that annual interest rate exorbitant, all customers would take advantage of a 2% discount (assuming they have the necessary cash available).

The same calculation process can be used to determine the approximate annual interest rate a business incurs for missing any early payment discount. Identify the number of credit terms within a year; then multiply that total by the percentage cost of each discount foregone. The final answer will not be precise, but it will indicate whether or not you should take a specific cash discount.

The following calculation provides a more accurate measure (we'll use a 365 day business year, instead of the standard 360 days employed in most of our calculations) of the annualized interest rate a business pays for the privilege of using a supplier's financing, that is, not taking a discount a supplier allows for early payment for purchases:

$$\text{Annualized Interest Cost} = \frac{\text{Discount Percent}}{(100\% - \text{Discount})} \times \frac{365}{(\text{Credit Limit} - \text{Discount Period})}$$

Using the 2% 10, net 30-day credit terms, we find:

$$\text{Annualized Interest Cost} = \frac{2\%}{(100\% - 2\%)} \times \frac{365}{(30 - 10)}$$

$$= \frac{2\%}{98\%} \times \frac{365}{20} = 37.2\%$$

A business pays an annualized 37.2% interest rate whenever it misses a 2% discount included on 2% 10, Net 30 Day selling terms. The same formula will determine the cost of missing a discount included in any firm's credit terms.

Table 9-3 lists the annualized percentage cost of missing the more common trade discounts.

Table 9-3

Cost of Missing Cash Discounts

Credit Terms	Annualized Percentage Cost
1/10, net 30	18.4%
2/10, net 30	37.2
3/10, net 30	56.4
1/10, net 60	7.4
2/10, net 60	14.9
3/10, net 60	22.6

Before missing a cash discount allowed for early payment, remember:

FINANCIAL FACT 14:

To measure the cost of missing a cash discount, translate it into its annualized interest rate.

A business can reduce the cost of missing a cash discount merely by delaying payment beyond the limit set by the seller's credit terms. For example, instead of paying for 20 days' credit consideration on 2% 10, Net 30 Day terms, you could defer payment for another forty days beyond the stated thirty day credit limit. The foregone discount then pays for sixty days in credit consideration. The extra forty day delay in payment lowers the 37.2% annualized interest cost to 12.4%. (Use the formula above to confirm that reduction.) However, meeting the limits set by a supplier's credit terms remains a prudent management practice. The business that abuses a supplier's credit consideration risks losing it altogether. Certainly that risk is more severe than the cost of paying within the supplier's maximum term.

Also note that the cost a business incurs from allowing discounts matches the cost paid by the business that skips those discounts. The business allowing a discount for early payment actually pays the buyer interest (in the amount of the cash discount) for the privilege of obtaining payment for the purchase more rapidly. For both the buyer and the seller, the financial view of cash discounts for early payment should become an important management consideration.

Credit Policies

Although credit terms exert a significant influence on a firm's operating results, it is unrealistic to assume that every customer will pay within the limit set by those terms. Some pay late accidentally; others pay late deliberately. Still others pay late because they simply lack the cash necessary to meet the seller's stated terms.

These unavoidable deviations make it imperative to recognize the impact a firm's credit policies have on its operations. After all, those policies set the standards that qualify customers for credit consideration. They directly affect sales, earnings, and the size of a firm's investment in accounts receivable.

Conservative credit policies preclude sales to customers who can't demonstrate the financial ability and management intention to pay promptly. Such policies hold down a firm's investment in accounts receivable and reduce its expenses from bad-debt write-offs. But conservative credit policies also reduce a firm's sales and gross profits.

Alternatively, liberal credit policies authorize sales to customers who clearly lack the ability to honor the firm's designated credit terms. That helps increase the sales and gross profits a business generates. But liberal credit policies also increase a firm's investment in accounts receivable and bad-debt expenses. Another look at Phoenix Company illustrates how these trade-offs influence the return a business generates from its assets.

We will assume that the company is exploring the potential benefits that might accrue from relaxing its present strict credit standards. Phoenix presently refuses sales to any prospective customer who lacks the ability to honor the firm's designated thirty day credit terms. That makes the firm's bad-debt write-offs nominal. But the policy also restricts sales to the $90,000 monthly volume shown in Table 9-1.

Logically, less restrictive credit standards should help increase the company's sales. The new sales will lead to a higher investment in receivables. But the company's existing customers presumably will continue to honor the standard requirement for payment in thirty days. At the same time, a portion of the new sales approved under the loosened credit standards will become bad-debt write-offs. Table 9-4 summarizes the Phoenix Company's analysis.

First, Phoenix established a set of credit standards that separated its existing and prospective customers into four groups. The most creditworthy (Class A) customers clearly display the financial ability to honor the firm's specified thirty-day credit terms. As noted above, that describes all of the company's existing customers. Competition precludes any additional sales to that customer pool. However, research suggests the following about the Phoenix Company's less creditworthy prospects:

1. Approving sales to Class B prospects will increase volume by $20,000 per month. On the average, Class B customers take 45 days to pay, while 2% of the sales to those customers will become bad-debt write-offs.

Table 9-4
Credit Standards and ROI
The Phoenix Company

Customers' Credit Quality	Payment History (days)	Monthly Sales	Bad-Debt Write-offs[a]	Investment in Accounts Receivable	Total Assets	Annual Earnings[b]	Return on Investment (ROI)
A	30	$ 90,000	—	$ 90,000	$500,000	$54,000	10.8%
B	45	110,000	4,800 (2%)	120,000	530,000	61,200	11.5%
C	60	130,000	7,200 (3%)	160,000	570,000	66,000	11.6%
D	90	150,000	9,600 (4%)	220,000	630,000	68,400	10.8%

[a]On incremental sales.
[b]Net of bad-debt write-offs.

2. Another $20,000 monthly sales increase can develop from sales to Class C customers. However, those prospects take 60 days to pay, while 4% of the volume will remain uncollectible.

3. Sales to Class D customers can provide still another $20,000 monthly boost to volume. Those customers defer payment for 90 days and a startling 4% of the volume will develop into bad debts.

As shown in Table 9-4, the standard ROI criterion suggests that the Phoenix Company should loosen its standards sufficiently to qualify Class B customers for credit consideration. That will boost the firm's ROI from 10.8% to 11.5%. Of course, sales to Class C customers will further boost the firm's ROI to 11.6%. But that slight increment isn't sufficient to overcome the margin of error inherent in the analysis. Extending credit to Class B customers marks the practical limit on the move to less restrictive credit policies for the Phoenix Company.

In no event should the company approve sales to Class D customers. The increase in receivables and bad-debt write-offs anticipated from that category erases the benefit the boost in sales provides to the firm's bottom line.

The outcome of the Phoenix Company's analysis is less significant than the approach. Presuming the necessary data are on hand, the approach can orient the construction of a firm's credit policies. Proper policies should contribute toward a higher return from the firm's assets.

Integrated Management Analysis

The discussion so far segments the management analysis of a firm's investment in accounts receivable. Realistically, you cannot focus on one segment while temporarily ignoring the others. All remain closely interrelated. That raises the need for integrated management analysis to recognize those interrelationships

The Gilbert Electronics Company provides an example. Gilbert presently generates $1.2 million annually in sales on 2% 15, Net 30 Day credit terms. Presently, 75% of Gilbert's customers take the 2% discount. Coupled with the nondiscount customer payment habits, that leaves the company with a 17-day average collection period and a $56,666 investment in accounts receivable.

Gilbert Electronics is considering changing its credit terms to 3% 10, Net 45 Days. Market research indicates that favorable customer response to the new terms will increase the firm's annual sales by $300,000. However, only 65% of Gilbert's customers will take the discount allowed for payment in ten days. The firm's average collection period will stretch to twenty days, and its investment in accounts receivable will rise to $75,000.

To justify the change, the proposed credit terms should increase the return from the company's assets. So we should note some additional facts about the firm's circumstances:

1. Gilbert's present $1.2 million sales volume generates $60,000 in annual earnings.

2. Those earnings represent a 15% return from the $40,000 average asset investment.

3. Disregarding any change in cash discounts allowed, Gilbert will realize a 7% net profit margin from the new sales, or $21,000 ($300,000 x .07).

4. The sales increase will not have any affect on the asset investment, other than the change in receivables noted above.

The first step in the integrated analysis determines how the proposed change in credit terms will affect the total cost of the cash discounts Gilbert Electronics allows for early payments.

Terms	Sales	% of Customers Taking Discounts	Total Cost of Discounts Allowed
3% 10, net 45	$1,500,000	65%	$29,250
2% 15, net 30	$1,200,000	75%	$18,000
Increase in Cost of Discounts Allowed:			$11,250

The new credit terms will increase the cost of the cash discounts Gilbert allows by $11,250 annually. That drops the contribution to earnings anticipated from the proposed change from $21,000 to $9,750. While that jump in earnings still appears significant, we cannot overlook the increase in assets that will accompany the new credit terms.

The only increase will appear in Gilbert Electronic's accounts receivable, which will increase from the present $56,666 level to $83,333. This will raise the firm's total asset investment to $426,667. Of course, the decision to implement the new credit terms hinges on the impact the change will have on Gilbert's ROI. So the total anticipated earnings must be related to the projected asset investment:

$$ROI = \frac{\$\ 69,750}{\$426,667} = 16.3\%$$

The proposed credit terms will increase the average return from Gilbert's assets from 15% to 16.3%. The new credit terms will be beneficial for the business.

Although in different circumstances the analysis might produce different results, Gilbert Electronic's analysis helps illustrate the premise found in:

FINANCIAL FACT 15:

Integrated management analysis should precede any change in a firm's credit terms or policies.

Changing credit terms without an integrated analysis may actually lower a firm's ROI, even though the change appears promising measured by the firm's earnings.

Chapter 10

Investment in Inventory

The need to have stock on hand to satisfy customer demand makes inventory a necessary asset. But a business should hold its investment in inventory to a minimum. This chapter reviews the fundamental formulas for analyzing the investment in inventory. Chapter 11 will establishes the management perspectives that help increase the return a business earns from that investment.

Formulas for Analysis

A sales forecast remains a necessary precedent for determining the proper size of a firm's investment in inventory. Presuming that a business begins with a realistic forecast, we can separate into three categories the components that make up that investment:

1. Sales stock

2. Safety stock

3. Expansion stock

Sales stock represents the foundation inventory a business needs to meet normal customer demand, perhaps measured by average daily or weekly customer purchases. Of course, customer demand seldom is completely predictable. An average daily or weekly sales total obscures inevitable fluctuations in customer purchase habits. On some days, purchases fall below the norm registered by the average. On other days, they rise well above the average level.

These inevitable fluctuations raise the need to add some safety stock to the inventory necessary to satisfy average daily sales requirements. Safety stock helps prevent the potential damage to customer relations and to future sales that can occur when a business lacks the inventory necessary to fill an order immediately.

The need for safety stock increases the total inventory, and total assets, a business needs to conduct its operations. That naturally exerts a downward influence on the ROI. But so long as that safety stock doesn't become excessive, the ability to satisfy fluctuating customer demand should contribute to earnings and overcome that downward influence while enhancing the ROI.

Safety stock also helps protect a business against unforeseen disruptions in supplier shipments. Even the most reliable supplier can encounter a wildcat strike, a winter storm, or a production breakdown that delays deliveries. The business without an adequate safety stock will lose profitable sales in the interim.

Finally, in an effort to increase sales, a business should add some expansion stock to its inventory requirements. If the anticipated increase in sales fails to develop, the extra expansion stock will reduce the firm's ROI. But any business pressing for a higher sales volume must accept that risk.

Two calculations provide the basis for analyzing a firm's investment in inventory:

1. Annual inventory turnover rate
2. Days' sales in inventory

The inventory turnover rate calculation measures how frequently a business recycles each dollar invested in its inventory during the year. More effective inventory management recycles each dollar more rapidly, reduces a firm's average investment in inventory, and increases its ROI. Determining the days' sales held in a firm's inventory provides another, more useful perspective for management. It measures the average shelf life for the items that make up a firm's inventory. Reducing that term improves a firm's operating results.

Annual Inventory Turnover Rate

An inventory item "turns" each time a business buys, sells, and repurchases another copy for stock. The number of times that cycle recurs during the business year represents that product's annual turnover rate. Analysts traditionally determine the average inventory turnover rate in a business as follows:

$$\text{Annual Inventory Turnover Rate} = \frac{\text{Annual Sales}}{\text{Average Investment in Inventory}^*}$$

*Or year-end investment in inventory

The annual inventory turnover rate for a business with $1,500,000 in sales and a $250,000 investment in inventory is:

$$\text{Annual Inventory Turnover Rate} = \frac{\$1,500,000}{\$\ 250,000} = 6$$

The business turns the average item carried in its inventory six times during the course of the year. Of course, not every item in the firm's stock turns at the same rate. Some cycle more rapidly, while others have a slower turnover rate. Effective inventory management looks at the annual turnover rate for each significant item included in a firm's stock. But the overall average provides a logical starting point for positive inventory management.

Note that the above calculation contains an inherent flaw. The sales total in the numerator includes the firm's gross profit margin—the markup over its product costs. So the calculation overstates the actual inventory turnover rate. A more accurate measure of a firm's inventory turnover rate uses the cost-of-goods-sold total (CGS) as the numerator. For example, if the above firm's cost of goods sold totaled $1,000,000 for the year, we find:

$$\text{Annual Inventory Turnover Rate} = \frac{\text{CGS}}{\text{Investment in Inventory}} = \frac{\$1,000,000}{\$\ 250,000} = 4$$

The firm actually turned its inventory four times during the year. Using the sales total in the numerator adds two nonexistent turns to the annual inventory turnover rate. That addition overstates the firm's turnover rate by 50%. The cost-of-goods-sold total in the calculation provides a more accurate measure for management. Many popular sources of comparative financial data continue to use the sales total in the calculation process. Consequently, if you are comparing your turnover rate with others in the industry, be certain you use the calculation consistent with that employed by your source of comparative data.

Table 10-1 offers a clear view of the direct relationship between a firm's annual inventory turnover rate and the size of its investment in inventory. It demonstrates that a more rapid turnover rate reduces the inventory level a business needs to conduct operations.

Table 10-1

Annual Turnover Rate
and Investment in Inventory

Annual Cost of Goods Sold

		$500,000	1,000,000	2,000,000	4,000,000
		Investment in Inventory			
Annual	2	$250,000	500,000	1,000,000	2,000,000
Inventory	3	166,667	333,333	666,667	1,333,333
Turnover	4	125,000	250,000	500,000	1,000,000
Rate	5	100,000	200,000	400,000	800,000
	6	83,333	166,667	333,333	666,666
	7	71,428	142,857	285,714	571,428
	8	62,500	125,000	250,000	500,000

For example, assume that a firm's annual cost of goods sold total $1,000,000. If the firm turns its inventory only twice during the year, it needs a $500,000 investment in inventory. Increasing the annual inventory turnover rate from two to three times a year lowers the inventory investment necessary to carry the same volume from $500,000 to $333,333. That frees almost $167,000 in cash for profitable reinvestment elsewhere. Another increase in the inventory turnover rate to four times a year lowers the necessary investment in inventory to $250,000 and frees cash that equals that investment.

A more rapid turnover rate translates into a smaller investment in inventory. Beginning with a target inventory turnover rate, use the following calculation to project the investment in inventory necessary to conduct any level of operations:

$$\text{Necessary Investment in Inventory} = \frac{\text{Projected Annual CGS}}{\text{Target Annual Inventory Turnover Rate}}$$

To illustrate, assume a business projects a $1,200,000 annual cost of goods sold total and expects to turn its inventory four times during the year. The necessary investment in inventory becomes:

$$\text{Necessary Investment in Inventory} = \frac{\$1,200,000}{4} = \$300,000$$

The calculation also helps identify the benefit a business gains from a more rapid inventory turnover rate. Stepping up the above firm's annual turnover from four to five times a year lowers its required investment in inventory:

$$\text{Necessary Investment in Inventory} = \frac{\$1,200,000}{5} = \$240,000$$

The more rapid inventory turnover rate lowers the necessary investment in inventory by $60,000. That reduction remains a desirable management objective, since a business increases its ROI whenever it reduces the total assets necessary to conduct any level of operations.

In any event, the other measure of a firm's investment in inventory—days' sales held in a firm's stock—makes a more direct contribution to the effort to control or reduce a firm's investment in that asset account.

Days' Sales in Inventory

Ideally, a business should begin each day with the minimum stock on hand necessary for that day's sales volume. This would eliminate any potential overinvestment in inventory. But few businesses can predict daily customer demand accurately. Moreover, few suppliers are able or willing to replenish a firm's exhausted stock daily. Most businesses carry inventory sufficient to meet anticipated customer demand for several days, weeks, or months.

The need to carry stock sufficient to accommodate fluctuating customer demand still doesn't justify an excess investment in inventory. A business should carry sufficient inventory, but not too much. To help achieve that balance, management should focus on the number of days' sales that a firm's inventory represents. A two-step calculation identifies that total.

The first step determines the average daily cost of goods sold (CGS)—the inventory that enters into a firm's daily sales. Using the financial data from the previous section, the calculation proceeds:

$$\text{Average Daily CGS} = \frac{\text{Annual CGS}}{360} = \frac{\$1,000,000}{360} = 2,777$$

The second step relates that average daily CGS total to the firm's investment in inventory:

$$\text{Days' Sales in Inventory} = \frac{\text{Total Investment in Inventory}}{\text{Average Daily CGS}} = \frac{\$250,000}{\$\ 2,777} = 90\ \text{Days}$$

The business carries an investment in inventory sufficient to satisfy its average daily sales requirements for 90 days. Table 10-2 shows that the size of a firm's investment in inventory shrinks as it reduces the number of days' sales carried in stock.

For example, assume that a business with a $1,000,000 annual cost of goods sold decides to carry stock sufficient for its normal sales requirements for 60 days. That raises the need for a $166,667 investment in inventory. However, the required investment will drop to $125,000 if management determines that stock for 45 days' sales is adequate to meet anticipated customer demand. Shrinking the required stock to a level sufficient for only 30 days' sales further reduces the required investment to $83,333.

Recognizing the number of days' sales in stock also provides some critical insight into a sensible inventory control program. A business manager easily can relate that number to the time required to order

Table 10-2

Days' Sales and Investment in Inventory

Annual Cost of Goods Sold

		$500,000	1,000,000	2,000,000	4,000,000
		Total Investment in Inventory			
Days'	30	$ 41,666	83,333	166,667	333,333
Sales	45	62,500	125,000	250,000	500,000
in	60	83,333	166,667	333,333	666,667
Inventory	75	104,166	208,333	416,667	833,333
	90	125,000	250,000	500,000	1,000,000
	120	166,667	333,333	666,667	1,333,333
	150	208,333	416,666	833,333	1,666,667

and receive (or produce) replacement stock. Thus the ability to replenish its stock rapidly shrinks the number of days' sales a business needs to maintain in inventory. Identifying the annual inventory turnover rate does not provide the same direct contribution to practical inventory management.

Remember this in:

FINANCIAL FACT 16:

Recognizing the days' sales a firm's stock represents provides the best perspective for inventory management.

The following chapter reviews some more tools that contribute to effective inventory management.

Chapter 11

Management Analysis: Inventory

A balanced investment in inventory remains essential for the business seeking the maximum return from its assets (ROI). However, achieving that balance can represent a formidable management challenge. A business must avoid an excess investment in inventory while still carrying stock sufficient to satisfy normal customer purchase requirements. This chapter reviews the analytic techniques that contribute to effective inventory management and help improve the total return a business generates from its assets.

Forecasting Inventory Requirements

A sales forecast stands as the starting point for effective inventory management. Ideally, that forecast proceeds from knowledgeable assessment of the projected economic environment and the anticipated influence that environment will have on a firm's market. Recognizing the constraints set by competition, a business then should forecast its annual unit sales volume and disperse it across operating periods, either weeks, months, or quarters.

Of course, every sales forecast contains a margin of error. Unpredictable fluctuations in customer demand are inevitable. But even a casual forecast provides some basis for controlling a firm's investment in inventory. The business that proceeds without a sales forecast loses that control

Figure 11-1 provides an idealized view of the contribution a sales

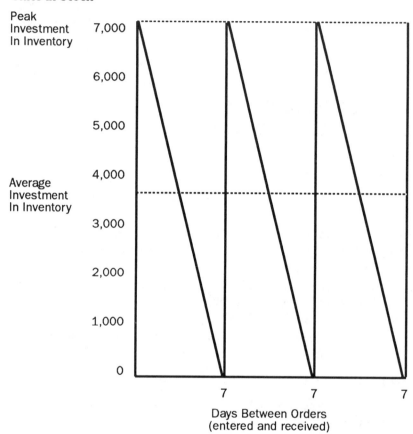

Fig. 11-1. Inventory control model. Days between orders as-sumes: 7,000 in weekly sales; 7,000 units is economic order quantity; 7-day order lead time.

forecast makes toward controlling the investment in inventory. Beginning with the premise that the business carries only one product, the view develops from several additional assumptions:

1. An accurate sales forecast projects a 7,000-unit weekly volume for the business, or a 1,000-unit average daily sales volume,

2. The economic ordering quantity for the business (illustrated later in this chapter) stands at 7,000 units,

3. Without fail, the firm's supplier makes delivery seven days after receiving each order,

As shown in Figure 11-1, the business marks the beginning of each seven-day inventory turnover cycle as it receives a 7,000-unit shipment from its supplier. The business simultaneously enters a new order for that amount for delivery seven days later. At the instant received, each 7,000 unit shipment represents the firm's peak investment in inventory.

The business then sells the inventory at the steady 1,000 unit daily rate over the seven-day period, exhausting its stock immediately before the next shipment arrives from the supplier. The steady sales rate and dependable supplier delivery habit enables the business to meet its sales forecast with a 3,500 unit average investment in inventory. This represents the average of the peak 7,000 units on hand at the beginning of each cycle and the zero level reached at the end.

The economic ordering quantity (EOQ) sets the minimum possible investment in inventory for the business. However, an accurate sales forecast is the necessary precedent for identifying that quantity and achieving that ideal management objective. A business operating without a sales forecast can easily carry either too much or too little inventory. Either circumstance damages a firm's operating results.

The critical contribution a sales forecast makes to the inventory control rates recognition in:

FINANCIAL FACT 17:

A sales forecast is a necessary precedent for controlling a firm's investment in inventory.

109

Of course, no business actually enjoys the balanced sales and supply circumstances of the firm illustrated in Figure 11-1. Businesses still need safety stock to meet unforeseen customer demands or occasional delays in supplier shipments. However, the need for safety stock does not alter the basic approach to controlling a firm's investment in inventory. Instead, the need for safety stock merely increases the size of a firm's average investment in inventory.

Figure 11-2 illustrates this fact. Here we presume that the business recognizes the inevitable margin of error inherent in its sales and delivery forecasts. As another assumption, sales will never exceed the 9,000 unit level in any week. Nor will the firm's supplier ever be more than two days late delivering any order.

These presumptions make the 2,000 unit safety stock in Figure 11-2 a sensible investment for the business. The need for that safety stock raises the firm's average investment in inventory to 5,500 units—the 2,000 unit safety stock plus its 3,500 average sales stock. However, the basic approach to controlling the firm's investment in inventory remains the same.

Economic Ordering Quantities

Given a sales forecast, the economic ordering quantity (EOQ) for a business determines the appropriate size of its average investment in inventory, but it seldom represents the minimum possible stock. Instead, a business should balance the increase in costs from more frequent orders against the cost benefits that develop from carrying a lower investment in inventory. The EOQ for a product minimizes the total of those two costs. That EOQ helps generate the highest return from a firm's assets.

The experience of the Marvel Motor Company demonstrates the process that identifies the EOQ for a particular product. Marvel operates as a regional distributor of electric motors to area manufacturers. During the upcoming business year, the firm expects to sell 16,000 units of a small replacement motor. Those sales will be evenly distributed throughout the year.

By entering one large order with its supplier, Marvel can begin the year with that total in stock. At the other extreme, Marvel can place sixteen orders for 1,000 units each during the year. Naturally, other order combinations also are possible between the two extremes.

Units in Stock

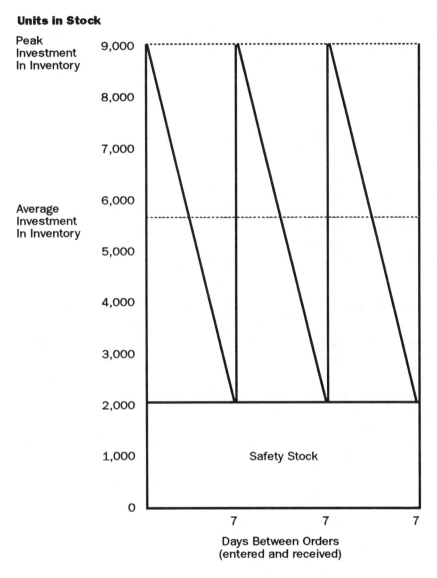

Fig. 11-2. Inventory control model with safety stock.

The $10 unit purchase price for the motors remains the same regardless of the quantity purchased in any order. So the analysis to determine the economic ordering quantity focuses on the trade-off between Marvel's inventory ordering and carrying costs. As the first step in that analysis, Marvel's management identified the relevant costs.

Ordering costs represent the costs a business incurs each time it orders inventory. Part of those costs arise from the clerical tasks necessary to write, process, and ultimately pay for each order. Another portion comes from the labor necessary to receive, verify, and shelve each shipment.

The cumulative ordering costs a business incurs usually remain approximately the same, regardless of the size of any order. Consequently, the business trying to minimize its ordering costs will enter the fewest number of orders possible. Marvel Motors incurs a $500 fixed cost from each order the firm enters.

Carrying costs represent the variable costs a business incurs from holding inventory in stock. That includes the obvious expenditure necessary to store and ensure a firm's inventory. Additional carrying costs arise from stock that deteriorates or becomes obsolete while it sits on the shelf unsold. Another component of a firm's inventory carrying costs arises from the cost of the funds invested in that asset. That component appears as a direct cost when a business uses borrowed funds to support its investment in inventory. But the business that doesn't borrow sustains a comparable opportunity cost from tying up its funds in inventory. The opportunity cost may be less apparent, but it remains nonetheless real. The Marvel Motor Company's cumulative carrying costs stand at 15% of the firm's average investment in inventory.

In any event, the total inventory carrying cost a business incurs is directly proportional to the size of its investment in inventory. To hold that cost to a minimum, a business should carry the smallest investment possible. But that increases the number of orders as well as the cumulative ordering costs. Consequently, the economic ordering quantity for a product minimizes the combined total of the inventory carrying and ordering costs a business incurs.

Table 11-1 shows how the Marvel Motor Company found the EOQ for its small replacement motors. First, management matched some alternative annual order frequencies with the order quantities necessary to fulfill the anticipated annual sales volume. Entering a single order for 16,000 units will hold Marvel's annual ordering cost to the $500 minimum amount possible. Smaller, more frequent orders naturally will increase the firm's annual ordering costs. Those costs will accumulate to the maximum total of $8,000 should the firm enter sixteen separate orders for 1,000 motors each. Smaller, more frequent orders also will reduce the size of Marvel's average investment in inventory.

To determine the averages employed in Table 11-1, Marvel's management proceeded from the two simplifying assumptions introduced at the beginning of the chapter:

1. Sales occur evenly throughout the year.

2. Each new shipment of replacement stock arrives at the instant the firm depletes its existing stock.

While both assumptions remain unrealistic, they still provide a sensible foundation for management analysis. Given those assumptions, dividing any order quantity by two identifies the average investment in inventory that will develop from that quantity.

In Marvel's circumstance, the average investment in small motors will peak at 8,000 units—and $80,000—if the firm enters only one order for 16,000 units. Table 11-1 shows that the firm's annual carrying cost for that stock will total $12,000 ($80,000 x 15%). More frequent orders will reduce the firm's annual inventory carrying costs. Those costs reach the $750 minimum if Marvel order 1,000 units sixteen times during the year.

The final step in EOQ analysis merely adds the ordering and carrying costs a business will incur from the alternative order quantities. The cost combination that minimizes that sum represents the EOQ for a product. Another glance at Table 11-1 indicates that the EOQ for Marvel's small replacement motors stands at 4,000 units. Either larger or smaller order quantities will raise the firm's total inventory costs above the $5,000 minimum that appears at that level. This point deserves emphasis in:

Table 11-1
Determining EOQ
Marvel Motor Company

Number of Orders (1)	Order Quantity (units) (2)	Annual Order Cost[a] (3)	Average Unit Inventory[b] (4)	Average Dollar Investment[c] (5)	Annual Carrying Cost[d] (6)	Ordering Cost plus Carrying Cost (7)
1	16,000	$ 500	8,000	$80,000	$12,000	$12,500
2	8,000	1,000	4,000	40,000	6,000	7,000
4	4,000	2,000	2,000	20,000	3,000	5,000
8	2,000	4,000	1,000	10,000	1,500	5,500
16	1,000	8,000	500	5,000	750	8,750

[a]$500 per order
[b](2) ÷ 2
[c](4) x $10
[d](5) x 15%

FINANCIAL FACT 18:

The economic ordering quantity (EOQ) for a product minimizes a firm's overall inventory costs.

A business should apply EOQ analysis to every product that represents a significant proportion of its sales.

At the same time, this approach to EOQ analysis can become tedious for the business that carries many products. Most managers will find the mathematical approach to EOQ analysis more appropriate.

The Mathematical Approach to EOQ Analysis

The mathematical approach to EOQ analysis relies on a standard financial formula:

$$EOQ = \frac{\sqrt{2SO}}{CP}$$

S = anticipated annual unit sales
O = fixed costs per order
C = annual inventory carrying cost, expressed as a percentage of the product's purchase price
P = unit purchase price for the product

Using the information from Marvel's analysis:

$$EOQ = \frac{\sqrt{2 \times 16,000 \times \$500}}{(15\%)(\$10)} = \sqrt{10,666,666} = 3,226$$

The economic ordering quantity for Marvel's small motors actually is 3,266 units. This falls below the 4,000-unit total previously identified. However, using a 3,200-unit quantity and five total annual orders as an example, we can confirm the accuracy of the mathematical approach:

Annual Ordering Costs (5 x $500)	$2,500
Annual Carrying Costs ($32,200 ÷ 2 x 15%)	2,400
Total Inventory Cost	$4,900

Ordering 3,200 units five times a year will make Marvel Motor Company's inventory costs $100 less than the apparent $5,000 minimum identified above. This demonstrates the potential value of the mathematical approach to EOQ analysis. The formula's simplicity and accuracy makes it an indispensable inventory management tool.

Quantity Discounts in EOQ Analysis

Both illustrations of EOQ analysis held the product's price constant. However, many businesses offer a lower unit price when a customer makes larger quantity purchases. Such discounts can change a product's economic ordering quantity. So, any potential quantity discounts should enter into the analysis that identifies a product's EOQ.

Quantity discounts can be included in the mathematical approach to EOQ analysis, but the necessary arithmetic adjustments become complex. So, we will use an alternative approach to see how quantity discounts enter into the approach to EOQ analysis introduced initially.

Table 11-2

Quantity Discounts in EOQ Analysis
Marvel Motor Company

Number of Orders (1)	Unit Order Quantity (2)	Price per Unit (3)	Quantity Discounts Foregone (4)	Ordering Cost plus Carrying Costs* (5)	Total Inventory Cost (6)
1	16,000	$ 9.50	—	$12,500	$12,500
2	8,000	9.75	$4,000	7,000	11,000
4	4,000	10.00	8,000	5,000	13,000
8	2,000	10.25	12,000	5,500	17,500
16	1,000	10.50	16,000	8,750	24,750

*From Table 11-1.

Assume that the price Marvel pays for its small motors depends upon the quantity purchased in any order. The unit price stands at $10.50

for order quantities of 1,000 or less. Then, as shown in Table 11-2, that price drops in twenty-five-cent increments as the alternative order quantities rise. Including all 16,000 motors in a single order will provide Marvel with a $9.50 minimum unit price.

The availability of quantity discounts doesn't alter the initial steps in EOQ analysis. The analysis begins by identifying the cumulative ordering and carrying cost a business will incur from alternative order quantities. After determining those costs, the analysis adds the additional expenses of foregoing any quantity discounts. The economic order quantity again becomes that which imposes the lowest total expenses on the business.

Here the quantity discounts raise Marvel's EOQ from 4,000 (or 3,200) units to 8,000 units. That ordering quantity will contribute toward higher earnings and a higher ROI.

The Reorder Point

Determining the EOQ for a product remains a futile exercise unless you also determine the proper time to place an order. Assuming a constant sales rate, the reorder point becomes:

Reorder Point = Lead Time in Days x Daily Sales Rate

To illustrate, assume that a business sells 5 units of a particular product daily. The firm typically waits ten days to receive purchases ordered. As soon as the firm's inventory level (less safety stock) reaches 50 units, the firm should reorder an amount equal to the product's EOQ. Presumably the order will be received when the firm's sales stock drops to zero. The safety stock provides the inventory necessary to absorb an unforeseen jump in sales or delay in delivery.

Inventory Accounting and ROI

Effective control of a firm's investment in inventory helps increase the return from its assets. However, the inventory accounting method a business employs also influences its ROI. In an apparent contradiction, the inventory accounting method that produces a higher ROI may not be the best alternative for a business. To illustrate that accounting contradiction, let's establish a common perspective of the two major alternative inventory accounting methods. That illustration centers on the experience of a small retail business, Autry Athletic Shirts.

Autry recently completed its first year in business. As an essential step in preparing the income statement for that year, Autry's accountant analyzed the store's inventory activity. Table 11-3 summarizes that analysis. Autry began operations with 1,500 athletic shirts in stock. The initial inventory cost $15,000, or an average of $10 per shirt. During the first six months in business, Autry purchased 6,000 shirts. However, the desire to upgrade the quality of the store's inventory, coupled with persistent inflation, drove the average price per shirt up to $12.

This trend continued during the second half of the year. Autry's cost averaged $14 for the 6,000 shirts acquired during the last six months. The store closed its business year with 4,000 shirts remaining in stock. The accountant used the information in Table 11-3 to determine the value of the firm's year-end inventory. He measured that value using both of the major inventory accounting alternatives.

Table 11-3

Inventory Activity: Autry Athletic Shirts

	Shirts	Average Cost per Shirt	Total
Opening Day	1,500	$10.00	$ 15,000
Purchases, first six months	6,000	12.00	72,000
Purchases, second six months	6,000	14.00	84,000
Total Available for Sale	13,500	12.66	171,000
Ending Inventory	4,000	*	*

* Values depend upon accounting alternative selected.

First, he calculated the store's year-end inventory value using the first-in, first-out (FIFO) method of accounting. FIFO accounting proceeds on the logical assumption that a business sells its inventory in the order acquired. The first item purchased from a supplier presumably becomes the first product sold to a customer. At the end of the business year, the firm values its unsold inventory at the cost of the last items acquired. Applying this principle to the 4,000 shirts on hand at Autry's year-end, FIFO accounting measured the value of that inventory: 4,000 x $14.00 = $56,000 FIFO assumes that all of

118

the unsold shirts on hand at the end of the year came from the 6,000 purchased during the last six months.

Second, the accountant measured the value of the same inventory using last-in, first-out (LIFO) accounting. LIFO proceeds on the premise that a business sells its inventory in reverse of the order actually acquired. The business theoretically sells its latest purchase before any like item previously held in stock. At the end of the year, the business values its unsold inventory at the oldest related costs.

Applying LIFO inventory accounting to the 4,000 shirts Autry held in stock at year-end, the inventory value calculation becomes:

Shirts		Cost Per Shirt		Total
(1) 1,500	x	$10.00	=	$15,000
(2) 2,500	x	$12.00	=	$30,000
(3) 4,000				$45,000

The LIFO calculation proceeds on the assumption that Autry's year-end inventory includes the store's opening day stock, plus the first 2,500 shirts out of the 6,000 purchased during the first six months of the year. Presumably, Autry sold none of these, but it sold all of the shirts purchased after the initial 4,000.

A two step process illustrates how the two inventory valuation methods lead to a different measure of the return from Autry's total asset investment. The first step compares the effects the alternative inventory values have on Autry's cost-of-goods-sold calculation. This is a necessary preliminary to the calculation of Autry's earnings below.

Both cost-of-goods-sold calculations (Table 11-4) begin with Autry's $15,000 opening day inventory. Both methods add the actual cost of the shirts acquired during the year to that opening day total.

Note that either method leads to the same value for the store's total inventory available for sale. Then each alternative subtracts the respective year end inventory values to determine Autry's cost of goods sold. From the discussion, we know that LIFO leads to an $11,000 lower value for Autry's closing inventory than FIFO. Here that translates into an $11,000 higher cost of goods sold for the year.

Table 11-4

Comparative Cost-of-Goods-Sold Calculations
Autry Athletic Shirts

	FIFO	LIFO
Beginning Inventory	$ 15,000	$ 15,000
Purchases (actual cost)	156,000	156,000
Total Inventory Available (at cost)	$171,000	$171,000
Less: Ending Inventory	(56,000)	(45,000)
Cost of Goods Sold	$115,000	$126,000

Before we complete the second step in the illustration, we should emphasize an important point. Neither accounting alternative effects any material change in Autry's inventory. The alternatives only lead to different accounting values for the same stock. That, in turn, affects the cost-of-goods-sold calculation as illustrated in Table 11-4.

To complete the illustration, let's see how the different cost-of-goods-sold values influence the measure of Autry's ROI. Those values exert that influence through the earnings calculation summarized in Table 11-5.

Note that FIFO accounting, with the lower cost-of-goods-sold total, leads to after-tax earnings $7,700 higher than those calculated with LIFO. Of course, higher earnings improve the return from a firm's asset investment. That holds true in this instance.

Before looking at the comparative ROI calculations, we should recognize another difference that develops from the alternative inventory accounting methods. Indeed, the lower ending inventory total produced by LIFO accounting affects a firm's balance sheet as well as its income statement. As that total reduces a firm's apparent earnings, it also shrinks its apparent asset investment. But that shrinkage seldom becomes sufficient to offset the depressing impact LIFO inventory accounting has on a firm's reported operating results.

Completing the illustration, assume that FIFO inventory accounting left Autry Athletic Shirts with $80,000 in assets—the $56,000 in inventory at actual cost plus $24,000 in other assets. LIFO account-

Table 11-5

Comparative Earnings Calculations
Autry Athletic Shirts

	FIFO	LIFO
Sales	$230,000	$230,000
Cost of Goods Sold	(115,000)	(126,000)
Operating Expenses	(80,000)	(80,000)
Earnings Before Taxes (EBT)	$35,000	$24,000
Tax Obligation (at 30%)	(10,500)	(7,200)
Net Earnings	$24,500	$16,800

ing lowers that asset total to $69,000 because of the lower accounting value of the firm's inventory. Now we can compare the overall influence each accounting method has on the apparent return from the firm's assets:

	Net Earnings	Total Assets	Return on Assets (ROI)
FIFO Inventory Accounting	$24,500	$80,000	31%
LIFO Inventory Accounting	$16,800	$69,000	24%

Since it produces a higher ROI, the FIFO approach appears to be the more desirable inventory accounting method for Autry Athletic Shirts. However, another look at the comparative income statements above argues against that assessment. While FIFO accounting produces a higher ROI, it also allows the tax system to drain more cash from Autry. Indeed, without affecting the physical composition of Autry's assets, FIFO accounting produces a $3,300 higher income-tax obligation. The business that finds cash more advantageous than a higher ROI will select the LIFO accounting method for its inventory.

One more illustration helps emphasize that fact. That illustration proceeds from the following assumptions:

1. Autry Athletic Shirts began operations with $25,000 in cash.

2. The store makes all sales for cash.

3. As a matter of policy, Autry pays cash for all purchases and operating expenses; the business defers no obligations in the form of accounts payable or accrued liabilities.

These assumptions help provide a clear view of the tangible cash benefit Autry gains from LIFO accounting. Table 11-6 provides that view with a look at the comparative cash flows that develop from the alternative inventory accounting methods. LIFO accounting leaves Autry Athletic Shirts with $11,800 cash at the end of the year—$3,300 more than that remaining should the business employ FIFO accounting. Autry must make a trade-off between the tangible benefit represented by additional cash and the management pride associated with a higher ROI. In this instance, Autry should accept the lower apparent ROI in exchange for the extra $3,300 in cash.

Table 11-6

Comparative Cash Flows
Autry Athletic Shirts

	FIFO	LIFO
Beginning Cash	$ 25,000	$ 25,000
Add: Cash Sales	230,000	230,000
Less: Purchases	(156,000)	(156,000)
Operating Expenses	(80,000)	(80,000)
Taxes	(10,500)	(7,200)
Ending Cash	$ 8,500	$11,800

In an inflationary environment, LIFO accounting actually provides a better perspective of a firm's "real" ROI because higher inventory replacement costs absorb a portion of the apparent gains from sales. When prices are rising, FIFO accounting overstates the real ROI a business produces.

You should consult an accountant before implementing any alternative accounting principles or procedures, but it's useful to recognize the cash benefits that a business can gain from LIFO inventory accounting. Moreover, as volume expands and inflation accelerates, the cash benefits from LIFO accounting increase.

Also recognize that any benefits from the original cash are enhanced by the warm glow any business manager feels when income tax obligations are reduced. That alone should compensate for the trauma associated with accepting a lower ROI.

Structural Analysis

Chapter 12

Liquidity in the Financial Structure

Few businesses grow and prosper without credit consideration, either in the form of trade credit from suppliers, or direct cash loans from banks or other financial institutions. Any credit consideration a business receives becomes a financial obligation. A business that fails to meet such obligations risks losing the opportunity to receive future consideration. That risk makes liquidity a major management concern.

Liquidity represents a firm's ability to meet its obligations on time. It often determines a firm's creditworthiness. It also helps protect against the management trauma that can develop when a business cannot meet its obligations on time.

A manager can view liquidity as a form of financial insurance. The more liquidity a business enjoys, the less likely a drop in sales, a strike, or some other business setback will lead to a financial crisis. Indeed, it provides a shield against financial failure.

From another perspective, excess liquidity has a negative impact on the return from a firm's assets (ROI). Assets held primarily to improve a firm's liquidity seldom make a significant contribution to that return. The business must make a trade-off between the financial protection that comes from liquidity and a higher ROI.

This chapter shows how liquidity enters into a firm's financial structure and influences the return from its assets.

Conceptual View of Liquidity

A business needs cash to meet its financial obligations. That makes a firm's cash balance an important factor in any measure of liquidity. From a creditor's viewpoint, a business should maintain cash on hand sufficient to pay all of its liabilities immediately. Of course, excess cash depresses a firm's ROI, just as any other asset overinvestment does. A business should carry sufficient cash, but no excess. That raises the need to add some other assets to any measure of a firm's liquidity.

Usually, that additional liquidity comes from a firm's investment in accounts receivable and inventory. As Figure 12-1 shows, it's easy to justify that addition since those assets revolve naturally through the cash flow cycle in a business.

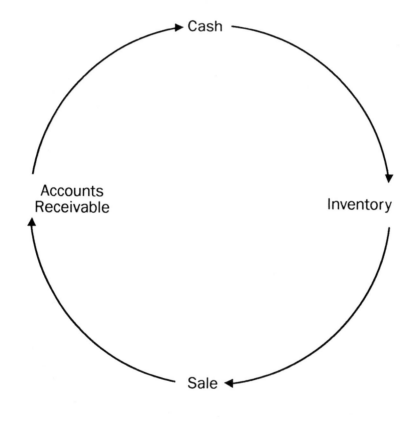

Fig. 12-1. The cash-flow cycle in a business.

Logically, the process begins with cash. Cash provides a business with the ability to purchase the inventory necessary for its operations, typically supplemented by trade credit consideration. The business then sells the inventory in exchange for accounts receivable from its customers. Collecting accounts receivable provides the cash the business needs to honor its obligations and continue the cycle. Of course, any disruption in the normal cash flow cycle reduces a firm's ability to meet its financial obligations promptly. A business cannot meet those obligations with uncollected accounts receivable or unsold inventory.

Even though the cash flow cycle revolves, an important distinction differentiates the relative liquidity represented by a firm's accounts receivable and inventory. Both represent liquid assets, since a business usually can convert either into cash within a relatively short period. But accounts receivable contribute more toward any measure of a firm's liquidity than inventory. After all, predictable customer payments automatically convert receivables into cash. But converting any inventory into cash requires a sale. Then a business must wait to collect the receivable that actually proceeds from that sale.

The need to sell inventory or collect accounts receivable places natural limitations on the immediate contribution those assets make to a firm's liquidity. Nevertheless, that contribution is valuable to the business trying to improve the return from its assets. Indeed, a business should make the cash flow cycle function as efficiently as possible. A more efficient cash flow cycle enhances the return from a firm's assets.

Practical View of Liquidity

The comprehensive measures of a firm's liquidity focus on the relationship between current assets and current liabilities. The Cradle Company's 12/31/90 balance sheet in Table 12-1 helps illustrate why that relationship is an important management concern.

First, note that the Cradle Company's cumulative investment in current assets—cash, accounts receivable, and inventory—totals $600,000 on 12/31/90. That investment represents the firm's *gross working capital*. Since its investment in current assets fluctuates directly in response to the prevailing level of its operations, a firm's gross working capital represents its "working assets."

129

Table 12-1

A Practical View of Liquidity
Cradle Company
12/31/90 Balance Sheet

Cash	$ 50,000
Accounts Receivable	250,000
Inventory	300,000
Total Current Assets	$600,000
Fixed Assets	200,000
Total Assets	$800,000
Accounts Payable	$250,000
Other Current Liabilities	150,000
Total Current Liabilities	$400,000
Long-term Debt	100,000
Total Liabilities	$500,000
Stockholder's Equity	300,000
Liabilities and Equity	$800,000

At any particular sales volume, the cash flow cycle in a business actually determines the total investment in gross working capital it needs to conduct its operations. Even the business that employs every dollar invested in its gross working capital as efficiently as possible must double that investment to handle a 100% increase in sales.

Of course, the concern here centers on the liquidity represented by gross working capital. Calculating the firm's net working capital provides one estimate of that liquidity.

Using the Cradle Company's financial circumstances, the calculation proceeds:

Gross working capital	$600,000
(Current Liabilities)	(400,000)
Net working capital	$200,000

The Cradle Company's net working capital provides a $200,000 liquidity cushion for the firm's short-term creditors. That cushion comes from current assets provided by long-term lenders and stockholder's equity, rather than by short-term creditors. From another perspective, the Cradle Company's total assets can shrink by $200,000 before the business loses the ability to meet its current obligations by liquidating those assets.

What constitutes a reasonable level of working capital naturally varies among businesses. The $200,000 level presumably appropriate for the Cradle Company may exceed or fall short of that appropriate for another business.

Unfortunately, because of size and volume differentials, external comparison to the level of net working capital held by other firms doesn't serve as a reliable management guideline. But introducing the basic working capital concepts here demonstrates the contribution liquidity makes to a firm's financial structure. We emphasize that contribution in:

FINANCIAL FACT 19:

The liquidity in a firm's financial structure enters into any estimate of its creditworthiness.

In any circumstance, a higher level of liquidity makes a firm more creditworthy.

Liquidity and ROI

Cash, accounts receivable, and inventory represent a firm's investment in liquid assets, although accounts receivable and inventory remain less liquid than cash. The cumulative investment in all three assets still contributes toward the general estimate of a firm's liquidity. The better that estimate, the more creditworthy a business appears.

Cash stands as a unique business asset. Prudent managers carry a cash "safety stock," although this contradicts the management precept that focuses on using a firm's assets as efficiently as possible.

A business easily can justify an investment in cash that exceeds the level set by its normal operating and safety stock requirements. That justification develops when the business encounters spontaneous opportunities for profit that require immediate cash payment. Of course, the profitable opportunities must occur frequently enough to offset the downward influence the extra cash has on a firm's ROI. Let's look at the trade-off that should orient the decision to carry extra cash.

Assume that a business seeks a 15% average return from its assets. This objective then stands as the minimum standard, or the "hurdle" rate, for justifying any arbitrary addition to that investment. The business encounters occasional but unpredictable opportunities for profit that require cash in excess of the balance necessary for normal operations. Some opportunities come from cash-short suppliers who offer unexpected cash discounts in exchange for early payments. Others arise from distress sales that require cash payment at the time of purchase. Still others develop from the bargaining strength a business gains when it has the capacity to offer immediate cash payment.

Whatever the sources, the business can use the 15% return standard to help estimate the additional cash investment warranted by the accumulated opportunities for spontaneous profits over the course of a year. An extra investment in cash makes sense when the anticipated contribution to the firm's incremental earnings represents no less than a 15% return on that investment. Table 12-2 demonstrates one approach that helps identify this beneficial "opportunity" cash.

Table 12-2

Opportunity Cash Analysis

Investment in Opportunity Cash	Anticipated Incremental Earnings	Return on Incremental Investment
$10,000	$ 5,000	50%
20,000	7,500	38
40,000	9,500	24
60,000	11,000	18
80,000	12,000	15
100,000	12,500	12

The investment-return relationships illustrated in Table 12-2 reflect the logical progression associated with increases in a firm's investment in opportunity cash: the incremental contribution to earnings and ROI shrinks as the level of opportunity cash rises. Table 12-2 also demonstrates the contribution the ROI standard makes to financial management. Increasing the firm's opportunity cash from $80,000 to $100,000 leads to higher earnings, but a lower ROI on the asset. The business that ignores the ROI standard may invest in assets (cash included) that increase its earnings while depressing its ROI. That fact notwithstanding, a business can benefit from an investment in cash that exceeds the level determined by its normal operating requirements. We mark that fact in:

FINANCIAL FACT 20:

A business often can justify an apparent overinvestment in cash.

Any apparent overinvestment in cash also enhances a firm's liquidity. The business becomes less susceptible to unforeseen setbacks that temporarily disrupt its normal cash flow cycle. That protection can make extra cash a wise investment, apart from the justification provided by potential opportunities for additional profits.

Cost of Inadequate Liquidity

Effective liquidity management can boost the return a business generates from its assets. However, that potential should not encourage an overzealous management effort that presses the limit on a firm's minimum liquidity requirements. A management error that leaves a business with inadequate liquidity can be costly.

For example, inadequate liquidity can make a business miss cash discounts that suppliers allow for early payment for purchases. It also may spoil the potential for spontaneous profits that require cash. Or it can even force a business to pay high interest rates for the borrowed funds necessary to meet immediate requirements for cash. The potential costs of inadequate liquidity should stand as a prominent management concern in any business. Too much liquidity can damage a firm's ROI. But too little can threaten its survival.

Chapter 13

Management Analysis: Liquidity

A business often can profit from an investment in liquidity that exceeds the level necessary to meet its predictable obligations. However, liquidity analysis focuses on the need to ensure that a business can meet all of its financial obligations promptly and preserve the credit consideration essential for the success of every business enterprise. This chapter introduces the analytic tools that help identify the liquidity a business should have in its financial structure.

Current Ratio

Liquidity analysis evaluates a firm's ability to meet its short-term financial commitments. The analysis focuses on the relationship between current assets and current liabilities. The *current ratio* provides the most direct measure of that relationship:

$$\text{Current Ratio} = \frac{\text{Current Assets}}{\text{Current Liabilities}}$$

Using the Cradle Company's financial structure presented in Table 12-1 as the basis for illustration, the firm's current ratio at 12/31/90 becomes:

$$\text{Current Ratio} = \frac{\$600,000}{\$400,000} = 1.5$$

The current ratio indicates that the firm has liquid assets sufficient to meet its short-term obligations 1.5 times.

The liquidity necessary to make a business financially sound varies among different industries. The 1:0 current ratio generally acceptable for a transportation company is unacceptable for most manufacturers and wholesalers. The proper evaluation of any firm's current ratio requires a look at the comparative industry standard, so we can't draw any final conclusions about the adequacy of the Cradle Company's liquidity.

The predictability of a firm's cash flow also has a significant influence on the current ratio appropriate for operations. A business that enjoys a predictable cash flow can operate with a current ratio that appears low compared to the industry standard. Alternatively, a business that has to contend with an erratic cash flow needs extra liquidity—and a higher current ratio—to maintain the ability to meet its obligations promptly.

Another useful perspective for evaluating a firm's current ratio focuses on the shrinkage in current assets a business can absorb before it loses the ability to cover its current liabilities:

$$\text{Current Asset Shrinkage Margin} \quad \left(1 - \frac{1}{\text{Current Ratio}}\right) \; 100\%$$

From the Cradle Company's financial structure, we find:

$$\text{Current Asset Shrinkage Margin} \quad \left(1 - \frac{1}{1.5}\right) \; 100\% = 33.3\%$$

The Cradle Company's current assets can shrink by 33% before the firm will find it impossible to cover its current liabilities. The shrinkage margin appropriate for a business again varies with the circumstances, but a higher current ratio and a larger shrinkage margin provide additional protection for a firm's creditworthiness.

Current Ratio Versus Net Working Capital

Chapter 12 introduced net working capital as a measure of a firm's liquidity and noted that a business cannot use the net working capital totals registered by other firms as comparative criteria for liquidity analysis. A simple illustration clarifies that limitation and provides another view of the contribution the current ratio makes to the analysis of a firm's liquidity.

Assume that two companies have matching $100,000 net-working-capital totals. That implies that the two companies enjoy a comparable level of liquidity. However, note that the equal net-working-capital totals come from the following current assets and current liabilities:

	Company A	Company B
Total Current Assets	$200,000	$1,000,000
Total Current Liabilities	(100,000)	(900,000)
Net Working Capital	$100,000	$100,000

The different magnitude of the two operations alters the presumption that the two businesses have a comparable level of liquidity. A look at the comparative current ratios for the two businesses makes that more apparent:

	Company A	Company B
Current Ratio	2.0	1.1

The comparative current ratios show that Company A enjoys a much higher level of liquidity. Since it accounts for the magnitude of an operation, the current ratio is the better indication of a firm's liquidity. We mark that fact in:

FINANCIAL FACT 21:

The current ratio represents the most common measure of liquidity in a business.

In the absence of industry comparative standards, a 2 to 1 current ratio presumably represents an adequate level of liquidity for a business. However, in any circumstance, another measure of a firm's liquidity also deserves attention.

Quick Ratio

A business with a current ratio that appears satisfactory still may not have an adequate level of liquidity. This apparent contradiction develops when the composition of a firm's current assets or current liabilities become unbalanced. Another comparative view of two businesses illustrates this potential problem:

	Company X	Company Y
Cash	$ —	$ 7,500
Accounts Receivable	—	7,500
Inventory	20,000	5,000
Total Current Assets	$20,000	$20,000
Accounts Payable	$ —	$ 5,000
Notes Payable	10,000	3,000
Accrued Liabilities	—	2,000
Total Current Liabilities	$10,000	$10,000
Current Ratio	2.0	2.0

The current ratios suggest that both businesses are equally liquid. But the composition of each firm's current assets and current liabilities makes it apparent that Company Y has a much higher level of liquidity. Company Y's cash and accounts receivable provide a significant degree of liquidity compared to Company X's single, relatively illiquid current asset in the form of inventory. Moreover, Company Y's liabilities represent a comfortable distribution of obligations compared to Company X's single liability. Company X's 2.0 current ratio clearly does not represent an adequate level of liquidity.

Such contradictions mean that the current ratio should be supplemented with a more stringent test of a firm's liquidity. The quick, or acid-test, ratio fills that need. The quick ratio is similar to the current ratio except that it excludes inventory from the measure of a firm's liquid assets:

$$\text{Quick Ratio} = \frac{\text{Cash} + \text{Accounts Receivable}^*}{\text{Current Liabilities}}$$

*Any marketable securities among a firm's current assets should be included in the numerator of the quick-ratio calculation.

Using the Cradle Company's financial position in Table 12-1 for illustration:

$$\text{Quick Ratio} = \frac{\$50,000 + \$250,000}{\$400,000} = .75$$

The contribution that the quick ratio makes to the management analysis of a firm's liquidity is self-evident. Inventory is generally a firm's least liquid current asset. By ignoring that asset, the quick ratio provides a better view of a firm's immediate ability to meet its obligations from cash and collections from customers. In fact, the liquidity implied by a high current ratio can disappear when a business also registers a low quick ratio. We recognize that fact in:

FINANCIAL FACT 22:

The quick ratio provides a stringent measure of liquidity in a business.

The traditional standard makes a 1 to 1 quick ratio mark an adequate level of liquidity for a business. But that again may well vary in a particular firm's circumstances.

Cash Ratio

The cash ratio represents the most stringent test of a firm's liquidity. That ratio relates the firm's current cash balance to its current liabilities. In the Cradle Company's circumstance:

$$\text{Cash Ratio} = \frac{\text{Cash}^*}{\text{Current Liabilities}} = \frac{\$\,50,000}{\$400,000} = .125$$

* Plus any marketable securities a business owns.

The Cradle Company has 12-1/2 cents in cash on hand relative to each $1 in current obligations. Unfortunately, no reliable comparative standard exists for determining the appropriate cash ratio for a business. Indeed, the ratio that provides a business with sufficient liquidity depends upon the characteristics of its own cash flow. At the same time, the business that recognizes those characteristics can use the cash ratio as a supplemental tool for liquidity management. That ratio standard should be set high enough to absorb unforeseen disruptions in cash flow.

Asset Activity Ratios

Complete management analysis of a firm's liquidity requires a look at the individual asset activity ratios introduced in Section Three. After all, a 2.1 current ratio may reflect an excess investment in inventory rather than an adequate level of liquidity. Similarly, a quick ratio that meets the traditional standard for adequate liquidity may develop from an over investment in accounts receivable that leaves a business short of cash. Comparative analysis of a firm's asset-activity ratios helps clarify or contradict the implications raised by the traditional liquidity ratios.

From another perspective, effective asset management may enable a business to operate with liquidity ratios that fall below any comparative standards. Thus a business with an inventory turnover rate that exceeds the industry average can operate with a lower relative investment in inventory. The smaller investment in inventory will reduce the firm's current ratio without impairing its liquidity. At the same time, effective credit and collection policies may reduce a firm's average collection below the industry average. The smaller investment in accounts receivable that results from those policies also will lower the firm's quick ratio. However, the lower quick ratio reflects effective asset management rather than inadequate liquidity.

A hasty conclusion based on the traditional liquidity ratios easily can be incorrect. The management analysis of a firm's liquidity also should recognize how individual asset accounts affect that assessment.

Chapter 14

Leverage in the
Financial Structure

Financial leverage from borrowed funds magnifies the impact that any change in a firm's earnings has on the return on stockholders' equity (ROE). This chapter illustrates that financial phenomenon. Chapter 15 will review the management analysis that should precede any decision to use financial leverage in a business.

Conceptual View of Leverage

Figure 14-1 helps illustrate how borrowed funds enter into a firm's financial structure and influence its operating results. Section A provides a conceptual view of the financial structure for a business that doesn't use any borrowed funds. Thus the stockholders' investment in the business is equal to its total assets. That makes the firm's balance sheet balance. However, the return on the stockholders' equity cannot exceed the return on assets. A 15% return on assets becomes a 15% return on the stockholders' equity. When a business doesn't use borrowed funds, an increase or decrease in its ROI produces a matching increase or decrease in its ROE.

Section B in Figure 14-1 includes some borrowed funds in the firm's financial structure. We can presume that the business uses the borrowed funds to replace a portion of the stockholders' equity, or, more commonly, that borrowed funds are used as an alternative to raising additional equity from stockholders. This view is more appropriate, since the advantageous use of financial leverage magnifies the return stockholders realize from any return on the firm's assets.

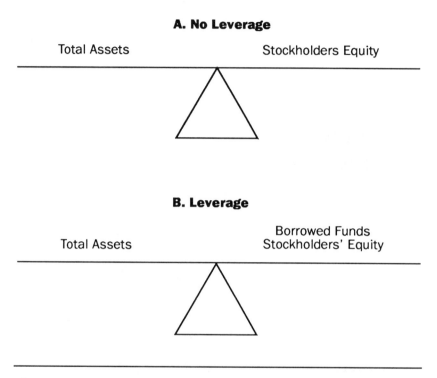

Fig. 14-1. A conceptual view of leverage.

For example, assume that the financial structure represented by Section B in Figure 14-1 includes equal amounts of debt and equity. The structure contains $1 in debt for every $1 stockholders have invested in the business. This debt naturally imposes interest charges that exert a downward influence on the firm's ROI. However, the earnings from the incremental assets easily can exceed the additional interest cost. And here the financial leverage enables the business to employ $2 in assets to provide a return for each $1 in equity. This doubles the ultimate benefit that stockholders realize from the net return from the firm's assets. A 10% return from the firm's assets translates into a 20% return on the stockholders' equity. A 15% ROI becomes a 30% ROE. The advantageous use of financial leverage magnifies the benefit stockholders gain from any particular return on a firm's assets.

However, we also must recognize that financial leverage magnifies the effects from negative operating results. Financial leverage exerts the same proportional influence on any loss that develops from a firm's operations. Thus the financial structure made up of equal amounts of debt and equity doubles the damage stockholders sustain from a firm's operating loss. An operating loss that represents a 5% negative ROI, translates into a 10% reduction in stockholders' equity. A 10% negative ROI becomes a 20% negative ROE.

Financial leverage magnifies the impact any firm's operating results have on the ultimate return those results represent for stockholders. A practical view of financial leverage clarifies that relationship.

Practical View of Leverage

A business with no financial leverage operates with an asset investment equal to the stockholders' equity. It produces a return on the stockholders' equity (ROE) that matches the return from its total asset investment (ROI). Naturally, any increase or decrease in the ROI will produce a corresponding increase or decrease in the ROE. However, a business can use financial leverage to increase its total asset investment well above the level supported by the stockholders' equity. Of course, stockholders enjoy the gain produced from all of a firm's assets, whether funded by debt or equity. The advantageous use of leverage magnifies the return on stockholders' equity that develops from any ROI.

The experience of the Home Computer Company demonstrates that financial influence. Home Computer is a new venture poised for entry into the booming personal computer market. Enthusiastically supported by a group of entrepreneurial investors, the proposed venture has the following financial characteristics:

1. The business needs a $1,000,000 total asset investment to operate profitably.

2. With those assets, the business will produce $250,000 in operating earnings during its first year in operation. (That excludes any potential interest expense.)

3. The investor group can fund the required assets with a $1,000,000 direct equity investment.

4. Alternatively, the business can initiate operations with as little

as $200,000 in stockholders' equity and borrow the funds necessary to finance up to $800,000 in additional assets.

5. Any borrowed funds will carry a 12% annual interest charge.

Using these characteristics as the basis for analysis, the investors focused on the return they could anticipate from four alternative financial structures for the Home Computer Company. Table 14-1 provides a comparative view of the four structures as well as a view of the net earnings, ROI, and ROE that would result from each alternative. It shows that Home Computer's first-year earnings and ROI will drop as the business increases the use of borrowed funds relative to equity. That drop isn't surprising since the firm's anticipated earnings before interest costs remain a constant $250,000, regardless of its financial structure.

If Home Computer operates with $1,000,000 in equity and with no debt, it will produce $250,000 in earnings and a 25% ROI. At the other extreme, coupling $800,000 in debt with $200,000 in equity reduces the earnings from the venture to $130,000 and the ROI to

---

Table 14-1

Advantageous Use of Leverage
Home Computer Company

Alternative Financial Structures

	1	2	3	4
Total Assets	$1,000,000	$1,000,000	$1,000,000	$1,000,000
Total Liabilities (15% annual cost)	—	200,000	500,000	800,000
Stockholders' Equity	1,000,000	800,000	500,000	200,000
Earnings before Interest Costs	250,000	250,000	250,000	250,000
Interest Cost	—	30,000	75,000	120,000
Net Earnings	$ 250,000	220,000	175,000	130,000
ROI	25.0%	22.0%	17.5%	13.0%
ROE	25.0%	27.5%	35.0%	65.0%

13%. Obviously, the difference in both instances arises from the $120,000 in interest charges that develop from that financial structure.

The drop in earnings and ROI induced by the interest costs suggests that borrowed funds are detrimental to the business. However, the comparative returns the investors can expect from the alternative financial structures contradict that assessment. In fact, as the investor group increases the use of borrowed funds, the return on each remaining equity dollar invested in the Home Computer Company rises. The financial structure with the minimum required $200,000 investment raises the anticipated return on stockholder's equity to 65%, which is well above the 25% ROE the investors can expect should they provide all of the funds necessary for the venture.

Presumably the investors seek the maximum possible return from their investments. So based on the analysis in Table 14-1, the Home Computer Company will initiate operations with the financial structure that requires the $200,000 equity investment and $800,000 in borrowed funds. That frees the investors' other funds for other profitable uses.

Here it is more significant to recognize how leverage magnifies the return a firm's ROI ultimately represents for stockholders. As illustrated in Table 14-1, that financial phenomenon easily can offset the depressing impact interest charges have on a firm's earnings and ROI. But keep in mind that the benefits stockholders can realize from borrowed funds are not automatic. Financial leverage also magnifies the negative impact a firm's losses have on the stockholders' equity.

Negative Effects of Leverage

The above analysis has proceeded on the assumption that Home Computer Company's first-year operating profits will total $250,000. Of course, this total may vary. Competitive pressure, management error, or an uncertain economy can make a firm's earnings fall well below those originally anticipated. In fact, instead of operating profitably, a business may sustain a loss.

Consequently, management also should recognize how financial leverage magnifies the impact an operating loss has on the stockholders' equity. Another look at the Home Computer Company illustrates that complementary analysis.

Assume that the investor group recognizes the potential for a maximum $200,000 first-year operating loss. Table 14-2 incorporates that prospect into the analytic format employed initially to illustrate the beneficial impact financial leverage has when a business operates profitably. But it also makes it apparent that financial leverage increases the damage stockholders' sustain when a business incurs an operating loss.

Table 14-2

Disadvantageous Use of Leverage;
Home Computer Company

Alternative Financial Structures
(from Table 14-1)

	1	2	3	4
Loss Before Interest Costs	($200,000)	(200,000)	(200,000)	200,000)
Interest Costs	—	(30,000)	(75,000)	(120,000)
Net Loss	($200,000)	(230,000)	(275,000)	(320,000)
ROI	(20.0%)	(23.0%)	(27.5%)	(32.0%)
ROE	(20.0%)	(28.7%)	(55.0%)	(160.0%)

The more financial leverage a business employs, the more severe the damage becomes. The same financial structure that produces the largest return on equity from a successful business imposes the largest penalty when a business operates unprofitably. Whenever a business incurs an operating loss, financial leverage makes a bad situation worse. Remember this in:

FINANCIAL FACT 23:

Financial leverage magnifies the return on stockholders' equity (ROE) that develops from any return on assets (ROI).

The following section provides a different perspective of that financial phenomenon.

146

Equity Multiplier

The business that uses no borrowed funds operates with a total asset investment equal to the stockholders' equity. By using borrowed funds, a business can expand that investment and increase the scope of its operations. Consequently, we can view financial leverage as an equity multiplier. Financial leverage enables a business to multiply its total asset investment above the limit set by the stockholders' equity.

Thus the business with the matching debt and equity totals has two dollars in assets working to provide a return for each equity dollar. Borrowed funds multiply the benefits any return on a firm's assets represent for each dollar committed by stockholders. In addition, that potential benefit can be measured directly. The first step identifies the specific equity multiplier at work in a business:

$$\text{Equity Multiplier} = \frac{\text{Total Assets}}{\text{Stockholders' Equity}}$$

To illustrate, the equity multiplier for a business with $300,000 in total assets and $100,000 in stockholders equity would be:

$$\text{Equity Multiplier} = \frac{\$300,000}{\$100,000} = 3$$

The business has three dollars working to provide a return for each dollar provided by stockholders. If the business produces a 10% return on its total assets, the equity multiplier magnifies the return that performance provides to stockholders as follows:

$$\begin{array}{ccc} \text{Return on} & = & \text{Return on} \quad \times \quad \text{Equity} \\ \text{Stockholders' Equity (ROE)} & & \text{Assets (ROI)} \qquad \text{Multiplier} \end{array}$$

$$\text{ROE} = 10\% \times 3 = 30\%$$

Since stockholders realize the net return from every asset dollar working for the business, the equity multiplier magnifies a 10% ROI into a 30% ROE.

Recognizing the equity multiplier in a business adds a new dimension to financial management. Holding its ROI constant, a business can increase the return on stockholders' equity by increasing its financial leverage and equity multiplier. It can provide a better return for its stockholders merely by increasing the use of borrowed funds. In fact, a high equity multiplier can transform an average earnings performance into an above-average return on the stockholders' equity.

Again, we must recognize the other side of this financial relationship. A higher equity multiplier also magnifies the drain on stockholders' equity created by any operating loss. For the example here, a 10% negative ROI will become a 30% negative ROE. A prudent manager recognizes both sides of the effect that the equity multiplier can have on a business.

Financial Limits on Leverage

Some natural financial limits exist on the benefits a business can derive from using borrowed funds. Exceeding those limits will lower the return a business produces for its stockholders.

One view of the natural limits on financial leverage focuses on the interest charges and incremental operating profits (EBIT) a business anticipates from any borrowed funds. Logically, leverage becomes beneficial only when the incremental operating profits exceed the interest charges. This circumstance produces higher net earnings and, ultimately, a better return on the stockholders' equity. Leverage becomes disadvantageous for a business whenever interest charges exceed the incremental operating profits.

Another view of the financial limit on leverage develops from a comparison of the interest rate attached to any proposed debt to the operating return on a firm's assets. As noted in chapter 7, the operating return on a firm's assets relates operating profits (EBIT) to total asset investment. For example, assume that a business produces $100,000 in operating profits from a $600,000 total asset investment. The operating return from the firm's assets becomes:

$$\text{Operating Return on Investment} = \frac{\text{Operating Profit (EBIT)}}{\text{Total Assets}} = \frac{\$100,000}{\$600,000} = 16.7\%$$

Since it ignores any existing interest charges, the operating-return-on-investment calculation provides a pure measure of a firm's ability to produce a return from its assets. At the same time, that return marks the limit on the interest rate a business should pay for any borrowed funds, since the cost incurred from a higher rate will exceed the operating return produced from the firm's assets. The cost will exceed the benefit. To employ financial leverage beneficially, a firm must generate an operating return on its assets that exceeds the cost of that leverage.

Chapter 15

Management Analysis: Leverage

The management analysis of financial leverage centers on three interrelated concerns. First, managers should recognize the financial relationships that make leverage beneficial for a business. Second, managers should recognize the risk that accompanies any borrowed funds included in a firm's financial structure. Third, prudent managers ensure that a business presents a sound financial appearance for its creditors. An excessive debt burden can discourage the approval of future credit consideration and hamper the growth and profitability of a promising enterprise.

This chapter reviews the management analysis that helps determine the financial leverage a business can use without incurring excessive risk or eroding the firm's ability to obtain credit.

Evaluating Leverage Risk

Any decision to use borrowed funds should proceed with the understanding that leverage imposes the risk of larger losses as well as the potential for higher earnings. That doesn't suggest that a business should never use borrowed funds. But the expected incremental earnings should justify the level of risk that accompanies the borrowed funds.

The Home Computer Company's circumstances illustrate one approach to evaluating that trade-off. But first let's clarify some implications from chapter 14. Home Computer's circumstances were designed to emphasize how borrowed funds can magnify the return a business produces on its stockholders' equity. Naturally, that relationship also holds true for a business already in operation.

But borrowed funds do not have to reduce a firm's earnings to produce a higher return on equity. Indeed, a business can use borrowed funds to simultaneously increase earnings and produce a higher ROE. After all, a business seldom increases its financial leverage merely to finance its current level of operations. Instead, a significant increase in debt usually precedes—indeed, anticipates— a projected increase in sales.

The process follows a logical course. A business projects a larger sales volume, either from a planned expansion into new markets, the introduction of a new product, or merely from a more aggressive sales effort. As a necessary precedent to the projected sales increase, the business must expand its investment in fixed assets and inventory. Using borrowed funds to finance the necessary asset expansion naturally increases the firm's financial leverage—the amount of debt in its financial structure relative to the stockholders' equity. Should the business subsequently achieve the projected sales increase, the anticipated rise in operating profits presumably will pay the cost of the borrowed funds and increase the ROE.

However, the uncertainty inherent in futurity makes risk an inseparable companion of borrowed funds. A projected sales increase that triggers an increase in a firm's financial leverage may or may not actually develop. But the interest charges that arise from borrowed funds are certain, and they represent the penalty a business must pay when it fails to achieve any objective originally used to justify an increase in its financial leverage.

Leverage risk analysis merely compares the projected benefits against the potential penalties that can develop from the different financial structures a business may employ. ROE represents the appropriate criterion for comparison. Table 15-1 illustrates that approach to comparative-risk analysis using the alternative ROEs developed for the Home Computer Company in chapter 14.

The analysis begins with a comparison of the two extreme outcomes possible from the four alternative financial structures originally considered. An initial glance at that comparison merely reminds us of the basic relationship summarized in Financial Fact 23: Financial leverage magnifies the ROE that develops from the ROI, whether the ROI represents the results of a profit or loss.

Table 15-1

One Approach to Financial Leverage Risk Analysis
Home Computer Company

Alternative Financial Structures
(from Table 14-1)

	1	2	3	4
Profitable Outcome	25.0%	27.5%	35.0%	65.0%
Unprofitable Outcome	(20.0%)	(28.7%)	(55.0%)	(160.0%)
Range	45.0%	56.2%	90.0%	225.0%

To gain a better comparative estimate of the risk associated with the four alternative financial structures, we must go a step farther and compare the ranges between the two extreme outcomes possible from each financial structure. Table 15-1 confirms that a larger range reflects a higher level of risk.

Excluding debt from Home Computer's financial structure will minimize the risk associated with the firm's projected operations. That financial structure holds the range between the best and worst possible outcomes down to 45%. As debt replaces larger portions of equity, the ranges between the two extreme outcomes increase. The maximum 225% range, the highest level of risk, develops from the financial structure that includes the maximum $800,000 in debt and $200,000 in equity.

Recognizing the risk that accompanies additional debt should encourage management prudence. A business should balance the higher return promised from additional financial leverage against the inherent risk. Unfortunately, the criteria for evaluating that trade-off are not well defined. What constitutes an acceptable level of risk in one circumstance may be inappropriate in another. Different business circumstances and different management dispositions create variations in the return necessary to justify any specific level of risk.

In addition, few businesses enjoy the relative certainty implied in the Home Computer Company's circumstance—that is, an equal chance for either $250,000 in operating profits or $200,000 in operating losses. Usually, a business confronts a wide variation of potential outcomes, and that makes any assessment of the risk associated with a project more difficult, although the basic considerations that enter into the analysis remain the same.

The fact that any financial leverage risk estimate is difficult only makes it more necessary. Even an uncertain risk assessment provides a better perspective for deciding whether or not a business should add leverage to its financial structure. The business that fails to make that assessment makes a serious management mistake.

Creditor Considerations

The potential return a business can gain from additional financial leverage often justifies accepting the associated risk. However, risk acceptable to a particular business may be unacceptable to its creditors. From a creditor's viewpoint, excessive financial leverage raises doubts about a firm's ability to meet its debt obligations over the long run. Too many doubts can disqualify a business from further credit consideration. So, the need to appear creditworthy may force a business to forego the return anticipated from additional financial leverage.

Trade creditors typically use some common analytic tools to evaluate a firm's creditworthiness. Some traditional standards set the limits on how much financial leverage a business can employ while still maintaining a creditworthy appearance. The business that observes those standards forfeits some of the potential return from higher levels of financial leverage, but it also enjoys a sound financial condition that contributes toward its long term survival.

The Happy Lamp Company illustrates the leverage analysis that qualifies a business for credit consideration. Table 15-2 provides a summary view of the relevant aspects of Happy's financial position and most recent year end operating results.

One measure of the Happy Lamp Company's creditworthiness comes from the *leverage ratio*. The leverage (or debt) ratio measures the proportion of a firm's total asset investment financed by creditors. The higher a firm's leverage ratio, the more debt it employs relative to the stockholders' investment in the business. That

154

Table 15-2

Leverage Analysis
Happy Lamp Company

Total Assets	$750,000
Total Liabilities	$500,000
(12% annual cost)	
Stockholder's Equity	$250,000
Liabilities and Equity	$750,000
Operating Profits (EBIT)	$125,000
Interest Charges	$ 75,000

translates into a higher level of financial leverage. A proportional relationship identifies the leverage ratio:

$$\text{Leverage Ratio} = \frac{\text{Total Liabilities}}{\text{Total Assets}}$$

Thus the Happy Lamp Company's leverage becomes:

$$\text{Leverage Ratio} = \frac{\$500,000}{\$750,000} = 66.6\%$$

The Happy Lamp Company finances two-thirds of its total asset investment with borrowed funds. Creditors usually consider that proportion as the traditional limit on the financial leverage a business can employ safely. A higher leverage ratio increases the risk that existing or prospective creditors associate with a firm's operations.

The *debt-to-equity* ratio provides a complementary view of a firm's debt burden. That ratio relates the borrowed funds a business employs directly to the stockholders' investment. To find the debt-to-equity ratio for the Happy Lamp Company, divide its total debt by the stockholders' equity in the business. In this instance, the calculation becomes:

$$\text{Debt-to-Equity Ratio} = \frac{\text{Total Debt}}{\text{Total Equity}} = \frac{\$500,000}{\$250,000} = 2$$

The Happy Lamp Company uses two dollars in borrowed funds compared to each dollar provided by stockholders. That corresponds to the 2:1 debt-to-equity ratio that marks the traditional limit on the debt a business should employ relative to the stockholders' equity. A business with a higher ratio often finds creditors reluctant to provide additional consideration. This limit on the financial leverage a business should employ deserves emphasis in:

FINANCIAL FACT 24:

A 2:1 debt-to-equity ratio marks the traditional limit on the financial leverage a business can safely employ.

This traditional limit isn't necessarily appropriate for every business. Complete comparative analysis also must recognize the standard for the industry in which a business operates. But a debt-to-equity ratio that exceeds the traditional standard usually raises questions about a firm's creditworthiness. Holding the ratio below that limit implies that a business enjoys prudent financial management.

Coverage Ratios

A satisfactory leverage or debt-to-equity ratio does not prove that a business has the ability to service its debts—that is, to meet its fixed payment obligations on time. Consequently, credit analysts complement the measures of a firm's financial leverage with a look at its coverage ratios. Coverage ratios relate a firm's operating results, measured by its income statement, to its fixed obligations. Those relationships provide essential estimates of a firm's ability to service its debt.

Times-Interest-Earned Ratio

The times-interest-earned (TIE) ratio relates a firm's operating profits to the annual interest charges that arise from its debt obligations. A higher ratio adds more certainty to the estimate of the firm's ability to pay all interest charges as agreed. The Happy Company's data from Table 15-2, show the times-interest-earned ratio for the business as:

$$\text{Times Interest Earned} = \frac{\text{Earnings Before Interest and Taxes (EBIT)}}{\text{Annual Interest Charges}}$$

$$\text{Times Interest Earned} = \frac{\$125,000}{\$75,000} = 1.66\%$$

The Happy Company produces operating profits sufficient to cover its interest obligations 1.66 times. Whether that provides an adequate coverage depends upon the stability of the company's operations. If sales and operating profits remain relatively stable, the ratio might indicate adequate coverage. However, a larger ratio may be appropriate to offset the unpredictability associated with a firm's operations.

Creditors traditionally look for a larger margin of error than that provided by Happy's 1.66 TIE ratio. A ratio of at least 2.0 generally is deemed necessary to provide appropriate assurance that a business can meet its interest obligations. A business with that ratio can sustain a 50% drop in operating profits and still retain the ability to pay its interest charges.

Fixed-Charge Ratio

Scheduled lease payments represent additional fixed obligations that a business must meet. The cumulative total of those obligations—lease payments plus interest charges—make up a firm's total annual fixed financial charges. The fixed-charge coverage ratio measures a firm's ability to pay those charges from the financial gains that develop from its operations. In that sense, the ratio becomes analogous to the TIE ratio. However, lease payments represent business expenses already deducted from sales revenue in the process that identifies a firm's operating profits, so those payments enter into both the numerator and the denominator of the fixed-charge ratio calculation:

$$\frac{\text{Fixed-Charge}}{\text{Ratio}} = \frac{\text{EBIT + Lease Payments}}{\text{Interest Charges + Lease Payments}}$$

Assuming that the Happy Company has $40,000 in annual lease payment obligations, we find:

$$\text{Fixed-Charge Ratio} = \frac{\$125,000 + \$40,000}{\$\,75,000 + \$40,000} = 1.43$$

The lease payments reduce the margin of error held in the Happy Company's operating results. Again, the appropriate ratio will vary among businesses and industries; but creditors and lessors become more comfortable as a firm's fixed-charge ratio rises toward the 2.0 standard for the TIE ratio.

Debt-Service Ratio

As emphasized in Financial Fact 6 in chapter 4, net income plus depreciation measures the annual cash flow a business generates. That measure becomes relevant here as an indication of a firm's ability to meet its fixed principal repayment obligations.

Principal repayments do not represent business expenses that flow through a firm's income statement. Instead, a business must generate an annual cash flow (after income taxes) sufficient to make those repayments. The relationship between annual cash flow and principal repayment obligations provides another measure of a firm's creditworthiness.

For example, assume that the Happy Company pays $10,000 in taxes on the firm's $50,000 in earnings after interest charges. That leaves the business with $40,000 in net income. Also, the business recognized $35,000 in depreciation expenses in its income statement and has $50,000 in fixed principal repayment obligations. We can find the firm's debt-service ratio as follows:

$$\text{Debt-Service Ratio} = \frac{\text{Annual Cash Flow}^*}{\substack{\text{Scheduled} \\ \text{Principal Repayment}}} = \frac{\$75,000}{\$50,000} = 1.5$$

*Net income plus depreciation.

The Happy Company's annual cash flow covers its principal repayment obligations 1.5 times.

The stability of a firm's annual cash flow naturally influences the debt-service ratio that it needs to appear financially sound. However, most businesses will need a 2.0 ratio to convince most creditors.

Profit Planning and Financial Forecasting Formulas

Chapter 16

Profit Planning
Formulas

The unpredictability of the marketplace affects the success of every business enterprise. Every business must contend with consumer whims, competitive pressures, and economic fluctuations. That uncertainty encourages many business managers to discard financial planning as a practical management tool. Presumably, an unpredictable future makes the planning effort futile.

But financial planning actually represents the *best* response to an unpredictable business environment. It makes management aware of the interrelationships that determine a firm's operating results. That awareness enables management to respond to unforeseen developments that may pose a financial threat to the firm. Financial planning also can help a business improve its operating results and strengthen its financial position.

This chapter discusses the basic profit planning process in a business. Chapter 17 will complement that discussion with a look at the forecasting method that anticipates changes in a firm's financial structure. Together, the two chapters provide the management foundation a business needs to contend with an uncertain environment.

Sales Volume and Operating Results

A rise in profits usually accompanies an increase in sales. Moreover, in most businesses, an increase in sales translates into a larger proportionate increase in profits. This financial phenomenon exists because a portion of the operating costs in most businesses are *fixed costs*. Those costs remain constant regardless of fluctuations in a firm's sales. For example, fluctuating sales seldom have an immediate impact on a firm's salary, lease, depreciation, or administrative expenses. Over any particular operating period, those expenses remain the same whether sales rise or fall. This magnifies the change in earnings that develops from any change in sales.

To illustrate the phenomenon, we also must recognize the other category of costs a business incurs. They come as variable costs. A firm's variable costs fluctuate directly in proportion with sales. A 50% increase in variable costs accompanies a 50% increase in sales. Product, packaging, and delivery costs exemplify the more common costs that fluctuate in line with a firm's sales.

Recognizing the distinction between the two categories of a firm's costs, let's examine a business that presently carries only one product, which sells for $10. The business incurs $2,500 in monthly fixed operating costs and a $5 variable cost from each unit sold. A 50% increase in sales from 1,000 to 1,500 units per month pushes up the firm's operating profits as follows:

Sales (units)	1,000	1,500
Sales (at $10 per unit)	$10,000	$15,000
Less: Variable Costs (at $5 per unit)	(5,000)	(7,500)
Less: Fixed Costs	(2,500)	(2,500)
Operating Profits (EBIT)	$ 2,500	$ 5,000

A 50% rise in sales translates into a 100% increase in operating profits. The larger proportionate increase develops since the firm's fixed costs remained constant as sales jumped. Consequently, the full $5 difference between the sales price and variable cost from each incremental unit sold proceeds directly into earnings.

Finance professors define this relationship as *operating leverage*. The definition arises from the premise that fixed costs leverage any sales increase into a larger increase in operating profits. This relationship has some important implications for financial management. A firm's operating leverage increases as fixed operating costs become a larger proportion of total costs. This expands the boost in operating profits that a business gains from any increase in sales. For example, assume that prior to the 50% sales increase the firm had increased its monthly fixed operating costs from $2,500 to $4,000. This enabled it to reduce the variable cost incurred from each unit sold to $3.50. The increase in sales from 1,000 to 1,500 units per month then would have had the following impact on the firm's operating profits:

Sales (units).................................	1,000	1,500
Sales (at $10 per unit)	$10,000	$15,000
Less: Variable Costs (at $3.50 per unit)	(3,500)	(5,250)
Less: Fixed Costs	(4,000)	(4,000)
Operating Profits (EBIT)	$ 2,500	$ 5,750

The 50% rise in sales translates into a 130% jump in operating profits. The higher fixed costs provided the firm with a higher degree of operating leverage (DOL). As a general criterion, the following relationship defines the DOL in a business at any time:

$$DOL = \frac{\text{Percent Change in Operating Profit}}{\text{Percent Change in Unit Volume}}$$

Using the most recent example to illustrate, we find the firm's DOL as:

$$DOL = \frac{130\%}{50\%} = 2.6$$

With the $4,000 in fixed costs, that 2.6 DOL tells us that any increase in sales above the 1,000-unit volume will induce a 2.6 times larger increase in operating profits. So, a 10% sales increase will boost operating profits by 26%. A 100% jump in sales will increase operating profits by 260%. The same proportionate operating leverage develops regardless of the size of the sales increase above the 1,000 unit level.

Conveniently, a firm's DOL can be measured without constructing the comparative income statements necessary for the calculation. This measure relates a firm's fixed costs to its current operating profits:

$$\text{DOL at X Units} = 1 + \frac{\text{Fixed Costs}}{\substack{\text{Operating Profits} \\ \text{at X Units}}}$$

Entering the data from above:

$$\text{DOL at 1,000 Units} = 1 + \frac{\$4,000}{\$2,500} = 2.6$$

This agrees with the DOL determined previously.

The opportunity to magnify the increase in profits that develops from any rise in sales suggests that a business always should employ a high degree of operating leverage. Presumably, fixed operating costs should represent a larger proportion of a firm's total costs at any sales level in order to enhance the gains realized from any subsequent rise in sales.

A high DOL often stands as a desirable management objective. But a high DOL also imposes additional risk on a business. As a high DOL multiplies the gains a business realizes from a sales increase, it also magnifies the financial damage that develops from any drop in sales. The same firm's circumstances helps illustrate that potential. But here let's assume that the firm's monthly sales volume drops from 1,000 to 500 units. The following comparison demonstrates how the 2.6 DOL magnifies the impact that a 50% drop has on the firm's operating profits:

Sales (units)	1,000	500
Sales (at $10 per unit)	$10,000	$5,000
Less: Variable Costs (at $3.50 per unit)	(3,500)	(1,750)
Less: Fixed Costs	(4,000)	(4,000)
Operating Profits (EBIT)	$ 2,500	($ 750)

The 50% decline in sales leads to a 130% decline in operating profits (50% x 2.6). Operating leverage exerts the same proportionate influence on the results that develop from a firm's sales fluctuations in either direction. Obviously, the business that seeks the gains available from a high DOL should not overlook the potential financial setback. The more unpredictable a firm's sales volume, the more undesirable a high DOL becomes. We can summarize that relationship in:

166

FINANCIAL FACT 25:

Fixed operating costs magnify the gains or losses that develop from any fluctuation in sales.

Note that interest charges from the debt a business uses aren't included in the fixed operating cost total used to determine operating leverage. Operating leverage focuses on the impact a change in sales volume has on operating profits—earnings before interest and taxes (EBIT). Of course, financial leverage magnifies the impact any change in operating profits has on a firm's net earnings. A high level of financial leverage benefits any business that increases its operating profits, but it also increases the penalty any business sustains from a drop in those profits.

Keep this relationship in mind when determining the degree of operating leverage to employ. A business with a high DOL should not simultaneously employ a high level of financial leverage. The combination makes the risk associated with a firm's operations too severe for a volatile economic environment. Alternatively, the business that functions with a low DOL often can accept a higher level of financial leverage. The lower risk associated with the DOL balances the higher risk associated with the financial leverage. These tradeoffs should determine how much financial and operating leverage to employ.

Break-Even Analysis

Fixed costs, both operating and financial, magnify the impact sales fluctuations have on a firm's operating results. At the same time, those costs usually are set as a business enters any particular operating period. Consequently, break-even analysis usually becomes the initial step in the profit planning process for each period.

Break-even analysis identifies the minimum sales volume a business must generate in order to avoid sustaining a loss. When a business achieves that volume, total sales equal total expenses. The business neither makes nor loses any money. Break-even operating results are never satisfactory, but the analysis can help management maintain and improve operating results.

Break-even analysis proceeds from the same division of a firm's total costs into the usual fixed and variable categories. However, it includes a third critical element—the contribution margin that develops from a firm's sales. This margin represents the difference between the sales price and the variable cost of a product. For example, assume that a product that has an $8 per unit variable cost sells for $12. The contribution margin from each sale is $4, the sales price minus the variable cost. The contribution margin included in each sale helps pay a firm's fixed costs and ultimately provides any earnings the business generates.

Profit planning focuses on the accumulated contribution margin anticipated from a firm's total sales volume. A business sustains a loss from its operations so long as the cumulative contribution margin from its sales remains insufficient to pay its fixed costs.

Alternatively, a business breaks even at that volume where the accumulated contribution margin from its sales equals its fixed costs. Identifying that point provides the foundation for the profit-planning process.

Finally, as a firm's sales rise above the break-even point, the incremental contribution margin proceeds directly to the bottom line. The business produces a profit.

Figure 16-1 helps to clarify the relationship between a firm's cumulative contribution margin. Figure 16-1(a) represents the unit sales price of a company's only product. That price is divided into its two component parts—the contribution margin and the variable cost. The square in Figure 16-1(a) represents the firm's total fixed costs, segmented into six equal units. Each subsection equals the contribution margin from a single unit sale of the firm's product. Note the relationship between the contribution margin and the firm's operating results as sales accumulate.

Figure 16-1(b) projects the results from a five unit sales volume. The cumulative contribution margin from that volume isn't sufficient to cover the firm's total fixed costs. The business sustains a loss equivalent to the contribution margin held in one unit sale.

An increase in sales from five to six units eliminates that loss. As illustrated in Figure 16-1(c), that sales volume generates a cumulative contribution margin equal to the firm's total fixed costs. Total revenue equals total expenses. The business breaks even.

Figure 16-1(d) demonstrates the result of sales that exceed the

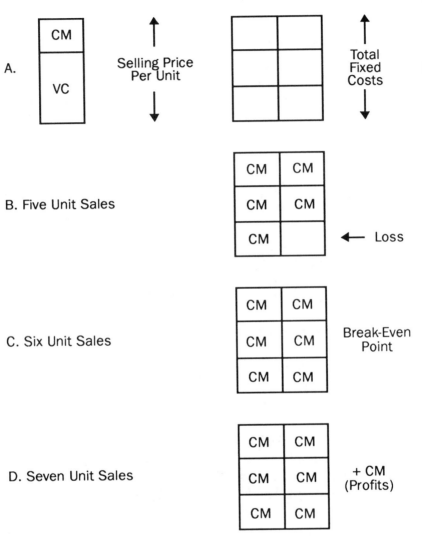

A.

CM

VC

Selling Price
Per Unit

Total
Fixed
Costs

B. Five Unit Sales

| CM | CM |
| CM | CM |
| CM | | ← Loss

C. Six Unit Sales

CM	CM
CM	CM
CM	CM

Break-Even
Point

D. Seven Unit Sales

CM	CM
CM	CM
CM	CM

+ CM
(Profits)

Fig. 16-1. Break-even analysis: a conceptual view.

break-even volume. An increase in the firm's volume to seven units creates earnings equivalent to the contribution margin from that incremental sale. The contribution margin from any additional sale also proceeds directly to the bottom line.

Calculating the Break-Even Point

The Local Company's simplified circumstances illustrate the calculations that identify a firm's break-even point. The Local Company carries only one product, which sells for $7 per unit, and it incurs $4 in variable cost from each unit sold. That makes the contribution margin from each sale $3. To break even, the company needs a cumulative contribution margin sufficient to cover the firm's $90,000 in fixed costs.

Given those facts, we can identify the Local Company's break-even sales volume:

$$\text{Break-even Unit Sales Volume} = \frac{\text{Fixes Costs}}{\text{Unit Contribution Margin}}$$

$$\text{Break-even Unit Sales Volume} = \frac{\$90,000}{\$3} = 30,000 \text{ units}$$

A 30,000-unit or $210,000 total dollar sales volume (30,000 x $7) provides the cumulative contribution margin necessary for the Local Company to break even. Each sale in excess of 30,000 units provides $3 in profit. Should the company sell fewer than 30,000 units, the cumulative contribution margin will fall short of the amount necessary to cover fixed costs. That will create a loss equal to $3 for each unit the firm drops below the break-even sales volume.

Lower fixed costs can reduce a firm's break-even point. Obtaining a larger contribution margin from each unit sale achieves the same objective. Of course, a larger margin can develop only from a higher sales price or a reduction in the unit variable cost. The break-even calculation provides a perspective that can help management seek better operating results. Remember that in:

FINANCIAL FACT 26:

Break-even analysis provides the foundation for profit planning in a business.

Most businesses carry a number of different products, and the various products typically have different sales prices, variable costs, and, consequently, contribution margins. Practical break-even analysis often requires a different calculation process. But the critical concepts do not change. A look at the Able Axle Company helps illustrate that process. A summary of its income statement shows that Able Axle presently operates profitably:

Sales	$275,000
Variable Costs	(87,500)
Fixed Costs	(140,000)
Earnings	$ 47,500

Management anticipates a downturn in the industry that will reduce the firm's sales. Before initiating any defensive management actions, it wants to identify the firm's break-even sales volume. However, costs and sales prices vary widely among Able Axle's products. No two products have the same contribution margin, so management cannot use the basic break-even calculation.

An alternative calculation, involving three steps, provides the same information. That calculation identifies the break-even sales volume that produces a cumulative contribution margin sufficient to cover a firm's fixed costs.

Using Able Axle's income statement, the first step identifies the total contribution margin accumulated from all sales.

Total Contribution Margin = Total Sales - Total Variable Costs

Total Contribution Margin = $275,000 - $87,500

Total Contribution Margin = $187,500

The second step determines the average contribution margin held in each sales dollar:

$$\text{Average Contribution Margin (per sales dollar)} = \frac{\text{Total Contribution Margin}}{\text{Total Sales}}$$

$$\text{Average Contribution Margin (per sales dollar)} = \frac{\$187,000}{\$275,000} \quad 68 \text{ cents}$$

The average Able Axle sales dollar contains sixty-eight cents in contribution margin. That amount out of each sales dollar contributes toward Able's fixed costs and, after those costs are covered, its earnings.

The third step uses the average contribution margin figure to determine the break-even sales volume:

$$\text{Break-even Sales Volume} = \frac{\text{Fixed Costs}}{\text{Average Contribution Margin}}$$

$$\text{Break-even Sales Volume} = \frac{\$140,000}{.68} = \$205,882$$

The Able Axle Company can sustain a $69,000 drop in sales and still produce break-even operating results.

This alternative approach to calculating the break-even sales volume in a business is useful in any circumstance. The only prerequisite is the need to delineate between a firm's fixed and variable costs.

One important assumption qualifies the results of this calculation process. The calculation presumes that the proportional product mix that makes up any sales volume holds constant as that volume fluctuates. Even though the product mix in a firm's sales varies from day to day, changes in that mix seldom induce significant changes in the average contribution margin. The individual fluctuations tend to dampen one another. Consequently, the three-step calculation process usually provides a reasonable management estimate of a firm's actual break-even point.

Target Profit Sales Volume

Since increasing profits from one operating period to the next remains an important measure of operating performance, a business often sets a predetermined level of earnings as an operating objective. With one change, the break-even calculation process identifies the sales volume necessary to achieve any target level of profits.

To demonstrate the calculation, let's assume that Able Axle's management wants to identify the sales volume necessary to generate $100,000 in earnings. The firm's fixed costs will remain constant, as will the average contribution margin held in each sales dollar. Management can use those facts to identify the sales volume necessary to produce the $100,000 target profit level:

$$\frac{\text{Target Profit}}{\text{Sales Volume}} = \frac{\text{Fixed Costs plus Target Profit}}{\text{Average Contribution Margin}}$$

$$\frac{\text{Target Profit}}{\text{Sales Volume}} = \frac{\$140,000 + 100,000}{.68} = \$352,941$$

Able Axle must increase its sales by $78,000 to generate $100,000 in earnings. A business that carries only one product can employ the same approach using the simpler calculation introduced initially.

The principles and procedures that enter into the profit planning calculations are relatively simple. But they remain only exercises in arithmetic until you employ the concepts to improve your firm's operating results.

Chapter 17

Financial Forecasting Formulas

The profit planning formulas in chapter 16 can help a business improve its operating results as measured by the income statement. But the financial impact from a firm's operations doesn't stop at the income statement. Those operations also exert a direct influence on the firm's financial structure found in its balance sheet. For example, the business projecting a significant increase in sales usually must expand its investment in inventory in order to meet the anticipated rise in customer demand. Moreover, an expansion in the investment in accounts receivable and other assets typically accompanies any increase in sales.

Since a balance sheet must balance, an increase in liabilities or stockholders' equity must match any expansion in assets associated with a rising sales volume. This fact makes financial forecasting a positive management complement to profit planning. Neither the amount nor the source of the funds necessary to support any increase in assets should come as a surprise. From another perspective, the failure to foresee the need for those funds can threaten a firm's financial integrity. This chapter illustrates the forecasting process that can help a business anticipate its financing requirements.

Dangerous Financial Gap

The effective financial manager anticipates the impact a firm's operations will have on its financial structure. That helps preclude damaging financial gaps. Those gaps can develop even in the business that operates profitably. A look at the Video Electronics Company demonstrates this potential financial problem.

Video Electronics distributes electronic computer games to department stores in its area. Table 17-1 shows the firm's financial structure as it stood at its 8/31/90 fiscal year end (FYE). That structure reflects the following characteristics about the firm's operations at that time:

1. A $2,500 average daily sales volume, coupled with a 50-day average collection period created the $125,000 investment in accounts receivable.

2. The $100,000 investment in inventory and $10,000 in cash represent the minimum amounts necessary for the firm's present sales level.

3. The $50,000 in accounts payable comes from one month's purchases; all of Video's suppliers expect payment thirty days after purchase.

4. Video Electronics earns $5,000 from each month's $75,000 sales volume.

The mushrooming popularity of electronic games is pushing up the demand for Video's product line. In fact, market surveys indicate that the company easily can double its $75,000 monthly sales volume. Since Video's fixed costs will remain constant, the 100% increase in sales will produce a 200% increase in earnings. The firm's earnings will jump from $5,000 to $15,000 per month.

Video's management decided to push for the higher sales volume. As the market surveys indicated, sales soon increased from $2,500 to $5,000 per day. Unfortunately, Video's management did not look past the operating results anticipated from the increase in sales. This shortsightedness opened the door to a severe financial problem. The natural expansion in assets from the higher sales volume created a large gap in the firm's financial structure.

Table 17-2 illustrates that gap with an imaginary view of Video's 11/30/90 balance sheet, three months after the decision to double the firm's sales volume.

Table 17-1

Video Electronics Company
(8/31/90 FYE Balance Sheet)

Cash	$ 10,000
Accounts Receivable	125,000
Inventory	100,000
Other Assets	40,000
Total Assets	$275,000
Accounts Payable	$ 50,000
Other Liabilities	25,000
Total Liabilities	$ 75,000
Common Stock	$ 50,000
Retained Earnings	150,000
Liabilities and Equity	$275,000

Table 17-2

Video Electronics Company
(11/30/90 Balance Sheet)

Cash	$ 20,000
Accounts Receivable	250,000
Inventory	200,000
Other Assets	80,000
Total Assets	$550,000
Accounts Payable	$100,000
Other Liabilities	50,000
Total Liabilities	$150,000
Common Stock	$ 50,000
Retained Earnings	195,000
Liabilities and Equity	$395,000
Financial Gap	$155,000
Total	$550,000

Look first at the asset section of the balance sheet. Since Video's operating characteristics remain constant, the increase in each asset account matches the 100% rise in monthly sales. The cumulative increase in assets totals $275,000.

Remember that the assets held in a firm's financial structure cannot increase independently. Video's liability and equity accounts must increase in some combination that matches and balances the $275,000 increase in assets.

A $75,000 increase in liabilities provided part of that necessary support. Accounts payable and other "spontaneous" liabilities typically fluctuate in line with a firm's sales. Here those liabilities doubled, matching the 100% jump in Video's sales rate.

Additional support for the higher asset investment came from Video's $45,000 in earnings ($15,000 per month) for the quarter ending 11/30/90. Since Video retained them, those earnings provided support for a matching amount of the increase in assets.

Nevertheless, the cumulative increase in Video's liability and equity accounts—$120,000—falls far short of the $275,000 total necessary to make the firm's financial structure balance. Table 17-2 isolates the shortage as a $155,000 imaginary gap in Video's financial structure. The foresighted business manager fills any anticipated financial shortage with borrowed funds or additional investment by stockholders. Alternatively, the business that lacks foresight will sustain a cash shortage and an excessive increase in accounts payable that violates supplier terms for payment. To avoid such problems, management must forecast a firm's financing needs and prevent any unforeseen gap in the financial structure.

Financial Forecasting Process

The process that anticipates a firm's financing requirements proceeds through five straightforward steps:

1. Express any projected sales increase as a percentage of the current operating period's, such as the current year, quarter, or month.

2. Multiply the existing investment in assets by the percentage sales increase anticipated during the upcoming operating period. This identifies the total asset expansion the business should expect.

3. Multiply accounts payable and accrued liabilities by the anticipated percentage increase in sales. This identifies the financial support for the asset expansion that will come from the spontaneous increase in liabilities.

4. Identify the increase in retained earnings expected during the upcoming operating period. This will equal the anticipated net earnings, less any dividend payment to stockholders.

5. Subtract the totals found in steps 3 and 4 from that found in step 2 to identify the net new financing requirements.

The Video Electronics Company's financial structure at its 8/31/91 FYE illustrates the financial forecasting process. As shown in Table 17-3, Video Electronics filled the $155,000 financial gap on 11/30/90 with a bank loan. The $15,000 in monthly earnings during the nine month interim to 8/31/91 reduced that loan to the $20,000 residual

Table 17-3

Financial Forecasting Process
Video Electronics Company
(8/31/91 FYE Balance Sheet)

Cash	$ 20,000			
Accounts Receivable	250,000			
Inventory	200,000			
Other Assets	80,000			
Total Assets	$550,000	x 50%	=	$275,000
Accounts Payable	$100,000			
Accrued Liabilities	50,000 } x 50%		=	(75,000)
Bank Loan	20,000			
Total Liabilities	$170,000			
Common Stock	$ 50,000			
Retained Earnings	330,000			
Liabilities and Equity	$550,000			
		Net increase in retained earnings	=	(125,000)
		Net New Financing Requirements	=	$75,000

amount remaining as a liability on 8/31/91. The firm expects to generate $2.7 million in sales during its fiscal year ending 8/31/92, which represents a 50% increase over the $1.8 million volume produced during the year ending 8/31/91. This expectation provides the basis for projecting Video's financing needs for 1992.

Multiplying the $550,000 in assets on 8/31/91 by 50% indicates that Video should anticipate a $275,000 increase in its total asset investment during 1992. The business will need an increase in liabilities and stockholders' equity in any combination that matches that asset expansion. Table 17-3 shows that Video can expect a $75,000 contribution toward the necessary financial support from the 50% expansion expected in its accounts payable and accrued liabilities. Presumably those liabilities will continue to expand spontaneously at the same rate as the firm's sales.

Video Electronics also expects to produce $250,000 in earnings from its $2.7 million sales volume in 1992. However, half of those earnings will flow out of the business as dividend payments to stockholders. Video will retain only $125,000 of its total earnings to help support its expected expansion in assets. Interrelating the above totals enables us to forecast Video's financing requirements for 1991 as shown in Table 17-3:

Anticipated Asset Expansion.. $275,000

      Less

Anticipated Spontaneous Increase in Liabilities .... (75,000)

      Less

Addition to Retained Earnings .... (125,000)

Net New Financing Requirements.................................. $ 75,000

Video needs $75,000 to maintain a balanced financial structure during the upcoming year. It may obtain the funds from an addition to its bank loan or perhaps from the sale of new equity.

Financial forecasting makes a critical contribution to a business by enabling management to foresee the need for new financing and avoid precipitating a financial crisis. The business gains time to arrange for the necessary financing or finds ways to reduce the need for financing. That contribution earns emphasis in:

That foresight also helps a business avoid financial difficulties.

Financial Forecaster's Perspective

Financial forecasting anticipates the asset growth associated with a projected increase in sales and then identifies the internal financial resources available to support the increase in assets. Should internal resources prove insufficient, the forecast measures the size of the potential gap in the firm's financial structure. A business can fill that gap with some form of external financing, either with additional debt or equity. However, external financing may not always be the best approach to filling a financial gap. Other management alternatives may eliminate the need for new financing.

For example, eliminating the scheduled dividend payments may eliminate Video's need for new financing. Or management might implement more stringent credit standards to reduce the firm's average collection period and erase a portion of the increase in receivables anticipated from a projected rise in sales. Alternatively, a more effective inventory control effort might reduce the need for the additional inventory necessary to provide for the sales increase.

Financial forecasting offers a valuable perspective. The manager who foresees the need for new financing gains the time to avoid a potential financial problem and also gains another justification for using the tenets of positive financial management.

Chapter 18

Financial
Management Formulas

All of the formulas and ratios discussed throughout this book contribute to positive financial management. Some help increase the profits a business generates. Others help a business employ its assets more efficiently. Still others reduce the risk associated with operating a business. But those analytic tools should not be applied randomly. Instead, a successful financial manager orients all efforts toward a managerial focal point. That focal point centers on the return a business generates from its assets—its ROI.

Return on investment provides a standard for evaluating how efficiently management employs the average dollar invested in a firm's assets, whether that dollar came from stockholders or creditors. Moreover, a better ROI also translates directly into a higher return on the stockholders' equity. Focusing on ROI also provides the basis for integrating many of the management concerns that influence a firm's operating results. The manager who focuses on ROI gains an advantage in the competitive environment. This chapter presents a summary view of the beneficial management perspective that develops from using ROI as the focal point for financial management.

Management Model

Figure 18-1 shows the critical financial interrelationships that determine the return a business generates from its assets. A glance at

Figure 18-1 shows that a firm's ROI results directly from the interrelationship between net profit margin and total asset turnover rate. The ROI a business produces represents the product of that interrelationship: the total asset turnover rate multiplied by the net profit margin equals the return on investment.

Some straightforward calculations provide a managerial perspective of Figure 18-1. One calculation identifies a firm's total asset turnover rate. A business that uses $500,000 in assets to generate $1,500,000 in sales determines its total asset turnover rate as follows:

$$\text{Total Asset Turnover Rate} = \frac{\text{Sales}}{\text{Total Assets}} = \frac{\$1,500,000}{\$\ 500,000} = 3.0$$

The business recycles the average dollar invested in its assets 3.0 times during the year. Analogous to the specific asset turnover rates in section 3, the total asset turnover rate stands as another measure of management efficiency. As management employs a firm's assets more efficiently, the asset turnover rate naturally increases.

Now, assume that the business produces a 5% net profit margin from its $1,500,000 annual sales volume. That leaves the business with $75,000 in net earnings. Using the original ROI calculation:

$$\text{ROI} = \frac{\text{Net Earnings}}{\text{Total Assets}} = \frac{\$\ 75,000}{\$500,000} = 15\%$$

We see that the business produces a 15% average return from its assets. However, a more useful perspective can be derived from the interrelationship presented in Figure 18-1. Expressing that relationship arithmetically, we find:

$$\text{ROI} = \frac{\text{Net Profit}}{\text{Margin}} \times \frac{\text{Asset Turnover}}{\text{Rate}} = 5\% \times 3 = 15\%$$

The two ROI measures agree. But the latter calculation stands as a more useful management tool. As projected in Figure 18-1, the calculation makes it apparent that management can increase a firm's ROI either by expanding its profit margin or employing its assets more efficiently. The business that may not be able to improve one

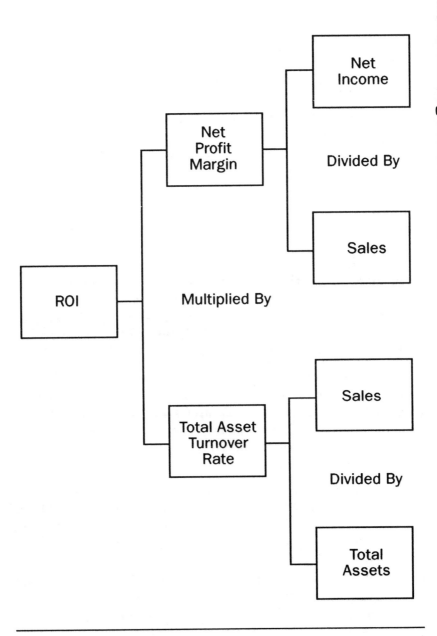

Fig. 18-1. The ROI management model.

element in the management model may be able to improve the other. Lets look more closely at those options.

Net Profit Margin

The net profit margin measures the average income a business extracts from each dollar in operating revenue. While total dollar profits remain important, the net profit margin indicates how efficiently a business operates. Better expense control creates a more efficient operation that produces a larger net profit margin and a higher ROI.

Expressing each major expense category as a percentage of its total operating revenue provides a useful approach to illustrating that potential. Figure 18-2 helps demonstrate that approach with a look at the operating results for the business described above, which presently has a 5% net profit margin. That margin represents the remainder after subtracting the firm's operating and nonoperating expenses from its total revenue. Naturally, reducing the expenses in either category will expand the firm's net profit margin. To provide a realistic estimate of that potential, the illustration expresses the underlying expense accounts as a percentage of sales.

The next level in the analysis separates the firm's total operating and nonoperating expenses into two categories each. Thus the product costs, the cost of goods sold, absorb 60% of the firm's operating revenue; selling and administrative expenses absorb another 20%. The firm's nonoperating expenses separate into interest charges equivalent to 10% of sales and taxes equivalent to 5%.

Even at this level, the potential benefits from this approach to analyzing net profit margin become apparent. First, the breakdown shows that the largest potential for improving the margin rests in the firm's cost-of-goods-sold account, the largest expense category. Logically, the effort to improve a firm's net profit margin should proceed in succession from the largest to smallest expense categories.

Figure 18-2 shows the beneficial impact a 10% reduction in the cost of goods sold—from 60% to 54% of sales—will have on the firm's net profit margin. The margin will increase dramatically from 5% to 11%. Of course, reducing any other expense category also will expand the net profit margin, but it will have a less dramatic impact.

Financial Management Formulas

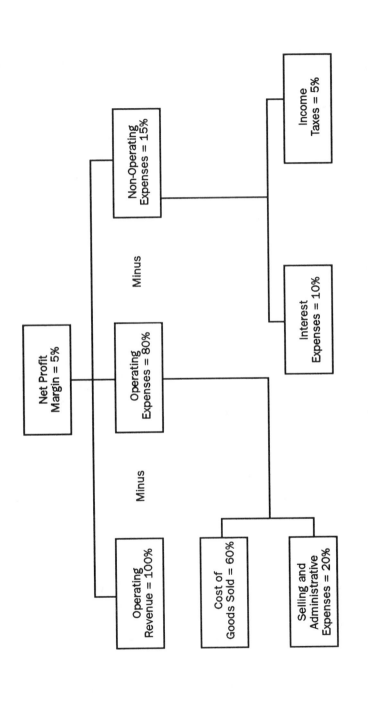

Fig. 18-2. The net profit margin in the ROI management model. All relationships are expressed as a percentage of the total operation revenue.

Management's analysis of any cumulative expense total should proceed to each successive level of the elements that enter into that total. Thus the next level of the analysis of the firm's cost of goods sold might develop as shown in Figure 18-3. This breakdown provides a more precise look at the potential expense reduction.

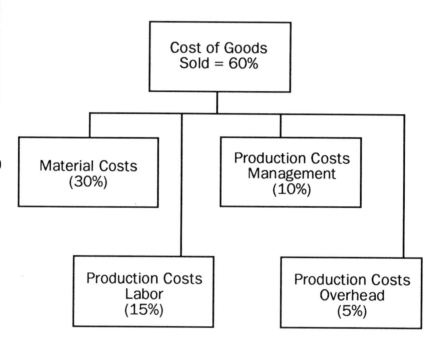

Fig. 18-3. Analyzing a firm's cost of goods sold.

The effort again proceeds in order from the largest to the smallest category of expenses included in the firm's total cost of goods sold, so here management should first explore the potential for reducing material costs. Any reduction in material costs will have the most significant impact on the firm's cost-of-goods-sold total and net profit margin. Management then should analyze the potential for reducing the other expenses included in the total cost of goods sold.

Logically, this analysis might look at the next level of underlying expenses included in each of the collective cost categories. Successive expense breakdowns may proceed through as many levels as make sense. In successive levels, this approach to analyzing a firm's net profit margin helps focus attention on the expenses that have the most significant impact on the firm's operating results. Any management action that reduces those expenses has the largest impact on the firm's net profit margin and ROI.

Holding the asset turnover rate constant, the following comparative relationships clarify the benefits of improving the net profit margin:

Asset Turnover Rate x	Net Profit Margin =	ROI
3.0	5.0%	15.0%
3.0	6.0%	18.0%
3.0	8.0%	24.0%
3.0	12.0%	36.0%

The effect a higher net profit margin has on a firm's ROI gains recognition in:

FINANCIAL FACT 28:

Expanding the net profit margin increases a firm's ROI.

However, as suggested in Figure 18-1, a higher net profit margin isn't the only path to a higher ROI.

Total Asset Turnover Rate

The other element in the basic management model recognizes the influence effective asset management exerts on a firm's ROI. A business that cannot expand its profit margin may still increase its ROI by employing its assets more efficiently. More efficient asset management reduces the total asset investment a business needs to conduct any level of operations. Holding any profit margin constant, the increase in efficiency will improve a firm's ROI, as well as the return on stockholders' equity, the ROE.

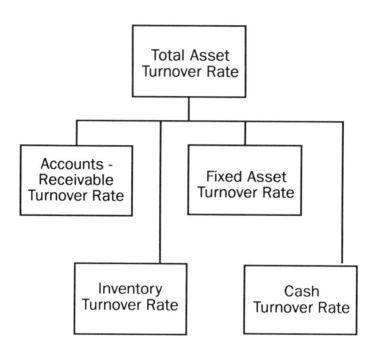

Fig. 18-4. Determining a firm's asset turnover rate.

To illustrate that potential, let's expand the basic ROI management model. Figure 18-4 shows that the total asset turnover rate develops from the interrelationship among the firm's individual asset accounts. Here we presume that the business has its $400,000 asset investment equally distributed among the four accounts, or $100,000 per account. Dividing the total investment into a $1,200,000 sales volume produces the firm's 3.0 total asset turnover rate. Presumably each individual asset account turns at the same rate.

Employing the dollars invested in any account more efficiently increases the firm's total asset turnover rate. For example, assume that more effective inventory management enables the same business to reduce its investment in that asset from $100,000 to $75,000. This reduction increases the total asset turnover rate to 3.2 ($1,200,000/$375,000), as well as increasing the firm's ROI. To demonstrate, let's assume that the business extracts the maximum possible 5% profit margin from its sales. More efficient asset management affects a firm's ROI as follows:

Net Profit Margin	x Asset Turnover Rate	= ROI
5.0%	3.0	15.0%
5.0%	3.2	16.0%
5.0%	3.6	18.0%
5.0%	4.0	20.0%

The initial increase in the firm's asset turnover rate increases its ROI from 15% to 16%. More rapid asset turnover rates push that return up further. We recognize this approach to increasing a firm's ROI in:

FINANCIAL FACT 29:

Increasing the total asset turnover rate increases a firm's ROI.

Improving a firm's asset turnover rate requires analysis of the underlying assets included in the major account categories. For example, a better accounts receivable turnover rate develops when a business presses slow paying customers for more rapid payment. And a better inventory turnover rate develops when a business manages that asset more efficiently.

At the same time, recognize that even if a business has a satisfactory ROI, both management analyses deserve attention. That holds true since a superior operating performance in one area can disguise a subpar performance in another. From a broad perspective, a business with a profit margin that exceeds the industry average may not be employing its assets as efficiently as possible. Alternatively, a higher asset turnover rate can obscure the potential for improving the net profit margin. The presumption that an acceptable ROI represents a satisfactory overall management performance will allow either deficiency to persist.

The same premise justifies the analysis of every successive level of the elements that determine a firm's net profit margin and total asset turnover rate. Specific operating expenses may be excessive even though a firm's net profit margin appears satisfactory. The assets held in a specific account may turn too slowly even though the firm's average asset turns at a satisfactory rate. Management should always proceed on the assumption that a good performance obscures the potential for improvement.

ROI and ROE

Chapter 7 illustrates the relationship between the return on asset investment (ROI) and return on stockholders' equity (ROE). A better ROI increases the ROE. Alternatively, any decline in ROI reduces the ROE. We recognize this important financial relationship in:

FINANCIAL FACT 30:

A firm's ROE fluctuates in direct response to any change in its ROI.

The changes will correspond exactly in the business that doesn't include any debt in its financial structure. After all, the stockholders' equity matches the firm's asset investment. The return on one account total must equal the return on the other. But few businesses operate without the use of borrowed funds. Since those funds magnify the impact any change in ROI has on a firm's ROE, leverage should be added to our view of the basic ROI management model.

Adding Leverage to the ROI Management Model

The equity multiplier (illustrated in chapter 14) measures the extent to which a business can benefit from using borrowed funds to finance some of its assets. A business that employs one dollar in debt for every dollar in stockholders' equity has an equity multiplier of two. In other words, it has two dollars in assets working to provide a return for every dollar stockholders have invested in the business.

This doubles the benefit stockholders realize from any positive return from those assets. But it also doubles the shrinkage in equity the stockholders incur from a negative ROI.

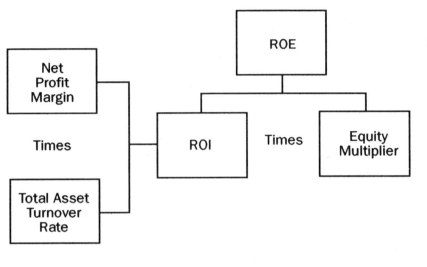

Fig. 18-5. Adding financial leverage to the ROI management model.

Any financial leverage magnifies the change in ROE that develops from any change in a firm's ROI. The equity multiplier increases whenever a business expands the proportion leverage occupies in its financial structure. Figure 18-5 demonstrates how the equity multiplier enters into the ROI management model.

Note that debt does not alter the basic relationship introduced at the beginning of the chapter. The ROI that a business generates still represents the product of the interrelationship between its net profit margin and total asset turnover rate. A better profit margin or a higher turnover rate improves a firm's ROI. Naturally, improvement in either area also produces a higher return for the stockholders' equity. However, Figure 18-5 makes it apparent that a higher equity multiplier also can improve the return stockholders realize from a firm's operations. We can summarize the cumulative financial interrelationships:

$$\begin{array}{ccccc} \text{Net} & & \text{Asset} & & \text{Equity} \\ \text{Profit} & \times & \text{Turnover} & \times & \text{Multiplier} & = \text{ROE} \\ \text{Margin} & & \text{Rate} \end{array}$$

or,

$$\frac{\text{Net Income}}{\text{Sales}} \times \frac{\text{Sales}}{\text{Total Assets}} \times \frac{\text{Total Assets}}{\text{Equity}} = \text{ROE}$$

The business introduced earlier demonstrates the complete financial interrelationship. That business produced a 5% net profit margin ($75,000) from its $1,500,000 annual sales volume. At the same time, it turned its $500,000 asset investment three times during the year. In the absence of any leverage, that translated the firm's profits into a 15% ROI and ROE.

Now we will assume that borrowed funds support half of the firm's asset investment. That makes the firm's equity multiplier two and produces the following impact on the return on the stockholders' equity:

Net Profit Margin		Asset Turnover Rate		Equity Multiplier		ROE
5%	x	3.0	x	2.0	=	30%

The equity multiplier in this instance doubled the benefit the stockholders gain from the firm's ROI. Indeed, a 15% ROI becomes a 30% ROE.

As the following comparison indicates, a higher equity multiplier increases the ROE that develops from any constant ROI:

ROI	x	Equity Multiplier	=	ROE
15.0%		1.0%		15.0%
15.0%		1.5%		22.5%
15.0%		2.0%		30.0%
15.0%		2.5%		37.5%

A high degree of financial leverage also can disguise an inadequate earnings performance or inefficient asset use. Indeed, a high equity multiplier can lead to an above average ROE even though a firm's actual operating results fall well below average. The business in such circumstances accepts an unnecessary level of financial risks.

At the same time, you should recognize the valuable management perspective that develops when you add leverage to the ROI management model. This offers a clear view of all of the interrelated financial factors that influence the return a business produces for its stockholders—earnings, asset use, and financial leverage. It becomes apparent that a poor management performance in any of the three areas will depress the financial return the business provides for its stockholders.

Recognizing how leverage affects the ROI management model completes the foundation necessary for an integrated approach to positive financial management. The business that uses this approach will increase its prospects for long term financial success.

Glossary

ACCOUNTS PAYABLE: Amounts due for purchases made on credit.

ACCOUNTS RECEIVABLE: A claim against a debtor for merchandise sold or services rendered in exchange for the customer's promise to pay on a later date.

ACCOUNTS RECEIVABLE TURNOVER: The net credit sales during a specific period divided by the average accounts receivable due from trade debtors; evaluates the quality of the accounts by relating the average total outstanding to the volume of credit sales.

ACCRUAL ACCOUNTING: An accounting method that recognizes sales when made and expenses when incurred, regardless of when the associated cash transactions actually occur.

ACQUISITION COST: The cost a business incurs from purchasing inventory, distinct from actual product costs.

ANNUAL CASH FLOW: The total of a firm's net income plus depreciation; the total measures the net incremental cash generated by operations over the course of a year.

ASSET TURNOVER: The ratio of total sales to total assets; a measure of the efficiency of asset utilization.

AVERAGE COLLECTION PERIOD: The average number of days each

credit sales dollar remains outstanding; a qualitative indicator of the collectibility of a firm's accounts receivable.

AVERAGE CONTRIBUTION MARGIN: Total sales divided by total contribution margin.

AVERAGE INVESTMENT PERIOD: The length of time each dollar remains in inventory before a sale converts it into cash or accounts receivable.

BAD-DEBT WRITE-OFF: The loss incurred when an open account sale proves to be uncollectible.

BALANCE SHEET: A financial statement that indicates what the firm owns and how those assets are financed in the form of liabilities and ownership interest.

BREAK-EVEN ANALYSIS: An analytic technique for studying the relationships among fixed costs, variable costs, and profits.

BREAK-EVEN CASH FLOW: The level of operations where total cash expenses equal total cash revenue.

BREAK-EVEN POINT: The volume of sales in a business where total costs equal total revenue.

CARRYING COSTS: Financial costs incurred directly or indirectly from carrying a firm's investment in assets.

CASH CAPABILITY: The total that comes from adding the firm's cash reserves to any available but unemployed credit consideration.

CASH CONVERSION PERIOD: The time lapse between the customer's decision to purchase a product and the date the payment for the purchase becomes cash available for reinvestment.

CASH FLOW CYCLE: The natural flow of cash through the operations in a business—cash to inventory to accounts receivable to cash.

CASH RATIO: Relates a firm's current cash balance to current liabilities; the most stringent test of liquidity.

COLLECTION PERIOD: See Average Collection Period.

COMMON-SIZE BALANCE SHEET: Expresses each account as a percentage of total assets or total liabilities and stockholders' equity.

COMMON-SIZE INCOME STATEMENT: Expresses each account as a percentage of total sales.

COMPONENT MANAGEMENT: The management effort that concentrates on control of the firm's investment in assets.

CONTRIBUTION MARGIN: Excess of sales price over variable expenses; an important element in break-even analysis.

COST OF GOODS SOLD: The cost associated with units sold during a specific time period.

COVERAGE RATIOS: Relates a firm's operating results measured by its income statement to its fixed obligations.

CREDIT POLICY: The guidelines used in the decision process that approves or disapproves of an open account sale.

CURRENT RATIO: Current assets divided by current liabilities; a measure of a firm's liquidity.

DAYS' SALES IN INVENTORY: See Average Investment Period.

DEBT/EQUITY RATIO: The ratio of the total debt to the total equity employed in a business.

DEBT SERVICE RATIO: Fixed principal repayments divided by annual cash flow (net income plus depreciation).

DEGREE OF OPERATING LEVERAGE (DOL): Percentage change in operating profits divided by percentage change in sales.

DEPRECIATION: A deduction of part of the cost of an asset from income each year of the asset's useful life.

EBIT: Earnings before interest and taxes.

EBT: Earnings before taxes.

ECONOMIC ORDERING QUANTITY (EOQ): The optimum (least cost) quantity of inventory that should be ordered.

EQUITY: See Stockholders' Equity.

EXPANSION STOCK: Inventory added to help increase sales for the business seeking a higher sales volume.

FIFO ACCOUNTING: A system of writing off inventory into cost of goods sold; items purchased first are written off first; referred to as first in, first out.

FINANCIAL STRUCTURE: The firm's balance sheet.

FIXED ASSETS: Relatively permanent assets used in the operation of a business.

FIXED ASSET TURNOVER: The result obtained by dividing the firm's sales volume by its investment in fixed assets; a measure of the efficiency in employing those assets.

FIXED CHARGE RATIO: Measure of the ability to pay annual fixed finance charges (lease payments and interest charges).

FIXED COSTS: Operating costs that remain constant regardless of the firm's sales volume; an important element in break-even analysis.

FYE: Fiscal year end.

GROSS PROFIT MARGIN: Cost of goods sold divided by sales.

GROSS WORKING CAPITAL: Cumulative investment in current assets—cash, accounts receivable, and inventory. Also called "working" assets.

GROWTH STOCK: That portion of the firm's investment in inventory designed to satisfy an anticipated increase in sales.

INCOME STATEMENT: A financial statement that measures the profitability of the firm over a period of time; all expenses are subtracted from sales to arrive at net income.

INVENTORY: Goods, purchased or manufactured, held by a business for sale.

INVENTORY/SALES RATIO: The proportional relationship between a firm's investment in inventory and its monthly sales volume; a criterion for controlling the firm's investment in inventory.

INVENTORY TURNOVER RATE: The cost of goods sold for a period divided by the firm's average investment in inventory; a measure of inventory management efficiency.

INVESTMENT: The funds a business invests in accounts receivable, inventory, and fixed assets.

ITEM ANALYSIS: The technique that isolates the turnover rate associated with the specific items that make up the inventory in a business.

LEVERAGE (OR DEBT) RATIO: Total liabilities divided by total assets. Measures the proportion of a firm's total asset investment financed by creditors.

LIFO ACCOUNTING: A system of writing off inventory into cost of goods sold; items purchased last are written off first; referred to as last in, first out.

LIQUIDITY: The ability of a business to meet obligations in a timely manner.

NET PROFIT MARGIN: Evaluates overall ability to squeeze profits from each sales dollar. Net profits divided by sales.

NEW WORKING CAPITAL: Current liabilities subtracted from gross working capital; provides an estimate of a firm's liquidity.

NIFO ACCOUNTING: Next in, first out accounting for inventory, which uses inventory replacement costs to record the cost of goods sold.

OPEN ACCOUNT SALE: A sale made in exchange for the purchaser's promise to pay on a later date; however, no promissory note is involved.

OPERATING LEVERAGE: Based on the premise that fixed costs leverage any sales increase into a larger increase in operating profits.

OPERATING PROFIT MARGIN: Deducting operating expenses (all costs incurred from normal operations, excluding interest charges and income taxes) from gross profits; the best measure of a firm's ability to make financial gains.

OPPORTUNITY CASH: Overinvesting in cash to increase earnings and enhance liquidity.

OPPORTUNITY COSTS: Earnings that might have been obtained if a productive asset, service, or capacity had been applied to some alternative use.

OVERINVESTMENT: Any cash committed to excess investment in accounts receivable, inventory, or fixed assets; or, extra assets unnecessary for the firm's level of operations.

PRETAX PROFIT MARGIN: Total sales divided by earnings before taxes (EBT); provides the best measure of actual earnings.

QUANTITY DISCOUNTS: Price reductions obtained by purchasing goods in larger lots.

QUICK RATIO: Similar to current ratio, but it excludes inventory from the measure of liquid assets.

RECEIVABLES/SALES RATIO: The proportional relationship between a firm's investment in accounts receivable and its monthly sales volume; a criterion for controlling the firm's investment in accounts receivable.

RETURN ON INVESTMENT (ROI): Earnings divided by average total assets; same as return on assets. A measure of the firm's asset utilization efficiency.

RETURN ON STOCKHOLDERS' EQUITY (ROE): The yield that earnings represent relative to the accounting value of the stockholders' investment, or net profits divided by the stockholders' equity.

SAFETY STOCK: Inventory held by a firm in excess of anticipated requirements to protect against unforeseen shortages.

SALES/FIXED-ASSET RATIO: See Fixed Asset Turnover.

SALES FORECAST: Projection of annual unit sales volume across operating periods, such as weeks, months, or quarters; used to control a firm's investment in inventory.

SELLING TERMS: The length of time a seller allows for payment of purchases made on credit; often includes discounts allowed for early payment.

STOCKHOLDERS' EQUITY: The total of common stock and all retained earnings.

STOCK-OUT COST: The opportunity cost that results from the inability to satisfy customer demand because of insufficient inventory.

STRAIGHT-LINE DEPRECIATION: A method of depreciation that takes the depreciable cost of an asset and divides it by its useful life to determine the annual depreciation expense; straight-line depreciation creates a uniform expense every year an asset is depreciated.

STRUCTURAL MANAGEMENT: The management perspective that seeks to maintain the proper balance among the elements that make up the financial structure in a business.

TARGET PROFIT SALES VOLUME: The average contribution margin divided by fixed costs plus target profits.

TIMES-INTEREST-EARNED RATIO (TIE): Relates a firm's operating profits to the annual interest charges from its debt obligations.

TOTAL CONTRIBUTION MARGIN: Total sales minus total variable costs.

TRADE CREDIT: Interbusiness debt that arises from credit sales; recorded as an account receivable by the seller and as an account payable by the buyer.

TRADE DISCOUNT: A deduction in the list price of goods allowed by a seller in return for payment within a specified time; for example, 2% 10, Net 30 Day terms allow a 2% discount from the list price if paid within ten days.

VARIABLE COST: A cost that is uniform per unit, but that fluctuates in total in direct proportion to changes in the related total activity or volume; an important element in break-even analysis.